Thinking About Ethics

RICHARD L. PURTILL

Western Washington State College
Bellingham, Washington

PRENTICE-HALL, INC., Englewood Cliffs, New Jersey

Library of Congress Cataloging in Publication Data

Purtill, Richard L 1931–
Thinking about ethics.

Bibliography: p.
Includes index.
1. Ethics. 2. Social ethics. I. Title.
BJ1012.P87 170 75–35672
ISBN 0–13–917716–7

Printed in the United States of America

10 9 8 7 6 5 4

Prentice-Hall International, Inc., London
Prentice-Hall of Australia Pty. Limited, Sydney
Prentice-Hall of Canada, Ltd., Toronto
Prentice-Hall of India Private Limited, New Delhi
Prentice-Hall of Japan, Inc., Tokyo
Prentice-Hall of Southeast Asia Pte. Ltd., Singapore

To my colleagues

Stan Daugert
Hugh Fleetwood
Phil Montague
Tom Downing
and
Hal Karason

in memory of many stimulating discussions
of ethical theories and problems

Contents

Preface vii

1

Ethical Relativism: Is Anything Wrong? 1

2

Egoism: Is It Human To Be Selfish? 16

3

Utilitarianism: The Greatest Good . . . 28

4

Ethical Rules: Love or Legalism? 40

5

Situation Ethics: Ethics Without Rules 53

6

The Sanctity of Life: At What Price? 67

7

Sexual Morality: Personal Relations 81

8

Sexual and Racial Discrimination: Are Some More Equal Than Others? 93

9

Ecology and Ethics: Do Trees Have Rights? 106

10

Ethical Motivation: How Should We Behave? 116

Additional Suggested Readings 128

Appendix: A Capsule History of Ethics 130

Subject Index 142

Index of Names 145

Preface

In an age which has seen Vietnam and Watergate, the fight for racial and sexual equality, and a revolution in sexual morality, it may seem strange to say that we do too little thinking about ethics. But in most cases our reactions to what might be called "moral crisis" are more instinctive and emotional than reasoned. There is a great deal of shouting, complaining, and losing of tempers about ethical problems, but very little *thinking* about ethics. Yet in our age we need to think more about moral problems than did those in previous ages. The modern, educated (or half-educated) person is not willing to accept the ethical judgments of others; the days of accepted moral authorities or even accepted community standards seem to be over. Furthermore, there are new problems which need thinking out even if we accept traditional starting points.

So we must think, and think hard, about our moral problems, and hope that thinking will be of some use. It is no use calling for "moral leadership" or hoping for a "return to morality" if we cannot agree on what morality *is*. Clearer thinking will not solve all of our problems, for morality is a matter of what we choose and not just what we think. But confusion is certainly no help in solving any problem, and once we begin to understand our problems better we may do a better job of making the right choices.

Two kinds of understanding are needed: understanding of morality in general, and understanding of particular moral problems. To understand morality in general, we need to look at the theories people have held about the nature of morality, and at the ways in which these theories can be justified. Earlier philosophers did not sharply separate this study of problems about morality in general from the study of particular ethical problems, as today's philosophers do. The study of the nature and justification of morality is often called *meta-ethics*. The first five chapters of this book deal with meta-ethics, because before trying to solve particular moral problems we must have some idea of what morality is and how moral problems are different from other problems.

Of course it is not enough just to clarify what the various theories are—we must also look at the theories and their assumptions critically and try to decide on the basis of argument which theory is the best one. But this job cannot be neatly separated from the jobs of looking at *specific* moral issues—war, racial justice, sexual behavior—and trying to come to some conclusions about them. So the second five chapters of this book deal with *normative ethics*, the study of particular problems *within* ethics.

The best way to start our thinking about moral problems is to start off with concrete cases. But real cases are highly complex and confusing, and involve numerous questions of fact. So I have taken a hint from some of humanity's great moral teachers and started with *stories* which make a point or suggest a question about morality. Taking these stories as a starting point I have tried to develop and discuss some theories about morality, and some answers to moral problems.

There are various ways in which this can be done, and one excellent way is an historical approach in which the ideas of the great figures of the past are examined and their pros and cons debated. But if this approach is used, the beginner in ethics may not be able to see the wood for the trees. So a better method for a first book in ethics may be to talk about ideas rather than about who held those ideas. This leads, perhaps, to some oversimplification, but once the beginner has the broad outlines he can go back and fill in the details by reading the great moral philosophers of the past. This book, at any rate, deals more with ideas than with those who held them, and I have tried to keep my discussions nontechnical without sacrificing accuracy.

Nevertheless, moral problems are complex and difficult, because human beings are complex and difficult to understand. Thinking about ethics is not easy; it requires all of our intelligence as well as all of our honesty and good will.

To act morally needs more than good will or intelligence; it often requires courage and determination. Self-discipline and practice are often necessary to carry out our moral ideals; the Greek philosophers who thought of morality partly as a set of habits established by repeated acts were recognizing an important practical aspect of morality. But thinking about ethics is rewarding, not only because it is a preparation for action, but also because moral problems are intensely interesting. They are part of the human condition, and to ignore the problems of morality is to fail to be fully human.

My thanks to the Bureau for Faculty Research at Western Washington State College for assistance in the preparation of this book; to Mrs. Mary Sutterman and Mrs. Ann Drake, who did the typing; and to Mrs. Jane Clark for her help with the proofreading. Thanks also to Norwell F. Therien, Jr., and Jamie Fuller of Prentice-Hall and to my students, my own teachers, and my colleagues, who have all in different ways helped make this book what it is.

Richard L. Purtill

1 Ethical Relativism: Is Anything Wrong?

Soon after Fred Perkins started college, he felt that he had thrown off the bonds of his upbringing in a small town. Especially, he felt that he was now liberated morally. Right and wrong, he now felt, were different for each person. If someone thought that something was right, it *was* right for him. No one could tell anyone else what he ought to do. This was especially true with sexual morality, Fred felt, and he thought of the narrow, self-righteous, hypocritical sexual morality of his home town as something he had definitely outgrown. Not that Fred had had much chance to put his theories into practice—he was a rather shy person and the few "swinging" girls he had met at college either didn't attract him or definitely scared him. But in theory he was for each person doing his own thing sexually.

When the rumors first started about college girls being raped in the little patch of woods near the main campus, Fred didn't think much of it. Some of his more advanced friends had told him that there was no specifically sexual morality, and it was the violence in rape that was wrong. But they seemed to justify violence in other cases, and Fred was confused.

But when he learned that Sue had been raped, Fred was very

upset. Not that Sue was his girlfriend or anything—she was just a girl whom he'd taken out a few times. But he saw her a few days after it had happened, and there was something about the way she looked and the fear in her eyes that caused a great rush of confused emotions in Fred. She looked sick and somehow ashamed. Fred wondered how well she would get over the experience and how it would affect her life. Suddenly the talk in the lounge of his dorm about how many times the rapist had scored, and whether the girls really enjoyed it, no longer seemed so funny.

Fred was now face to face for the first time with an action he really felt was evil—not something in a book or a newspaper, not something on the TV screen, but something that touched him personally. And he began to think about his own moral theories. His parents, he knew, and the people in his home town would say without hesitation that what the rapist had done was wrong, and that he should be punished. But what if the fellow thought that what he was doing was right? Didn't that make it right for him? Fred began to think of the protest rallies against the war that he had attended with his friends. Most of these friends agreed that it was up to each individual to decide what was right for him. But they had no hesitation in condemning the President and the South Vietnamese as murderers, as corrupt, as oppressors and exploiters. How could you say that nothing was wrong unless the person doing it thought it was wrong and still condemn people as evil? Didn't everyone think that what he was doing was right? Then how could anything be wrong?

Fred didn't come to any very definite conclusions when he began thinking about these things. He thought that perhaps he ought to change his moral principle from "nothing is wrong unless the person thinks it is," to "nothing is wrong unless it hurts people." But there were so many ways of hurting people. Joe down the block was really sick when Fred got the scholarship to State that he and Joe had been competing for. And then there was this rapist. Fred had a feeling he should be punished. But wouldn't that hurt him and therefore be wrong? Fred came to the conclusion, which somehow comforted him, that the rapist was insane and should be cured, not punished.

But not long after that a fellow in Fred's class named Harry gave himself away as the rapist—he couldn't help hinting and boasting when he was drunk. Harry! *He* never had any trouble getting girls, though the way he treated them he sometimes had trouble keeping them. But, he boasted to Fred, there was a thrill

> in forcing a girl. Sue, now, she'd squeaked like Minnie Mouse when he grabbed her. Fred knew he wasn't lying—he remembered that little shrill squeak Sue gave when she was frightened. All of a sudden he found himself punching Harry right in the face. Harry slipped and fell down the flight of stairs nearby. He lay at the bottom groaning, with his leg at a funny angle and blood on his face. But more than Harry was in ruins: Fred's newfound conclusions were wrecked, too. He was glad he'd hit Harry's sneering face and put him out of action for a while. And he was sure Harry wasn't insane—just selfish, mean, and bad.

Many people today have ideas about right and wrong like those that Fred started out with. Not all of them have their convictions tested so dramatically, but many of them sooner or later come up against things which they want to condemn morally, only to find that their moral theory gives them no ground for doing so. There are many things which we could do in a situation like this. We could give up trying to be consistent; we could rush from one extreme to another, following our emotions. But if we try to apply our intelligence to the situation, there are certain questions we will need to ask. Just what does it mean to say that what's right for each person is what he feels is right? How much truth is there in this idea? What reasons do we have for holding it or rejecting it?

When we try to answer questions like these, we are engaging in Ethics or Moral Philosophy. In one way, no one is forced to deal with questions like this; he can accept his answers from the society around him or from some authority. But even that requires a moral decision: you must decide to go along with the society around you or decide to obey some authority. And these days the society around us speaks with divided voices, and almost every authority is challenged. Decisions about how to live, how to treat other people, are difficult and complex. We can, if we like, try to shirk such decisions or let them be made for us by chance. But since such decisions can affect our whole lives and play a major part in whether we are happy or unhappy, it would be silly not to use all of our intelligence and common sense in arriving at such decisions. Someone who spends a great deal of time or attention choosing clothing or records or sports equipment, but accepts any ready-made moral ideas that happen to be floating around, is nothing less than a fool.

One of the shoddier pieces of moral merchandise, which a good many people accept without much examination, is this idea that "right is what each person thinks is right." In the first place it takes a little doing even to make sense of this view. Suppose that I am trying to explain Japanese society to you and I tell you that the concept of an *on* is extremely important. You ask me what an *on* is and I tell you, "Each person has an *on* if he thinks he has an *on*." You would very rightly object that I hadn't told you much. What does "having an *on*" *mean?* Does it make you laugh or make you cry? How does it affect what you do or don't do? About all the description tells me is that an *on* is something subjective; having an *on* is not like having five dollars or having a broken leg, because in those cases having the thing is different from thinking you have it.

Suppose I explain that in Japanese society if someone does you a favor you have an *on* towards that person, and that you will feel that you must do him an equal favor in return. You now have some idea of what an *on* is; you can relate it to English expressions like "being under an obligation" or "owing someone a favor," and have some idea of the circumstances under which people will feel they have an *on*.

But once you realize this, you will find it hard to believe that having an *on* is purely subjective, purely a matter of feeling that you have an *on*. Surely if you are ever under an obligation, you are under an obligation to someone who, for instance, saves your life. Surely you can't get out of an obligation just by not feeling it, or put yourself under an obligation to someone who has done nothing for you simply by feeling that you have one? In other words, the concept of being under an obligation is not purely subjective, but has connections with facts, such as the fact that A has saved B's life.

Of course there are some concepts that are purely personal and subjective. You can like a person, for instance, whether he has done anything for you or not, whether he has qualities other people admire or not. But even a vague general feeling of liking has some connections with such things as behavior. If you claim to like a person, but avoid him completely, never do the slightest thing to please him, and so forth, what does your claim to liking the person amount to? A *purely* subjective concept, one with *no* connections with facts or behavior, would be useless. We could not learn how to use it, and would not know how to apply it.

Suppose, however, that when someone says, "right is what each person thinks is right," he means "right is what each person approves of." The danger here is that "approve" can mean a great many things. It can mean "to regard as right or good," which would bring us right back to the definition of "right" we just criticized. Or it can just mean "to feel favorable toward." Feeling favorable toward something might mean simply that you had certain interior feelings or it might mean that you acted in certain ways. Suppose that we define approving something as acting in certain ways to that thing. Then to say that Harry was right to rape Sue would be to say that he thought it right, which would be to say that he approved of it, and *that* would be just to say that he chose to do it. In other words, no one could ever be said to do anything wrong, because to say that it was right for him to do a thing would just be to say that he had chosen to do it.

But this just doesn't seem to be the way people ordinarily talk about right and wrong. It seems to make perfectly good sense to say, "He thought that it was wrong, but he did it anyway," or "He was aware that it was right, but he refused to do it." Also, almost everyone has had the experience of doing something which he believed to be wrong, or not doing something he believed to be right. Of course this feeling that what we are doing is wrong *may* be based on a mistaken idea, and the way people talk about right and wrong may be based on some sort of confusion. Experience is sometimes misleading; common ideas or ways of speaking are sometimes confused. But it takes an argument to convince us that experience and common practice are mistaken. And what argument is there to show that right actions are simply the actions people in fact choose, and that nothing is ever really wrong?

Some arguments that people use in this connection seem to be based on confusion. For example, people argue, "You must follow your conscience, and this means that only you can determine what is right or wrong for you." It *is* a truism that each person must follow his conscience. But this simply means that after you have gone through whatever process you go through in order to determine whether something is right or wrong, you must act on the basis of this determination. In just the same way, when a doctor has gone through whatever processes he goes through to arrive at a diagnosis, all that he can do is act on the basis of that diagnosis. In other words it is of no use to tell him to act on the basis of the *right* diagnosis. He can only act on the basis of what he *believes* to be the right diagnosis and hope that his belief is correct. But there is often a difference between what *is* the right diagnosis and what a given doctor *believes* is the right diagnosis. Now there may also be a difference between what a person believes is right to do on a given occasion and what *is* right to do on that occasion. The fact that all we can do is act on what we believe to be right does not settle the issue one way or the other, for that is all that we can do in any kind of activity.

Some defenders of moral subjectivism give the argument that right and wrong are purely subjective because there are no agreed-on ways of settling questions about right and wrong. Whether a doctor's diagnosis is right or wrong is a matter of fact, which can be settled. But, it is argued, whether an action is morally right or morally wrong is merely a matter of opinion and cannot be settled.

Let us take a look at this argument. We must be very careful that we don't compare very simple matters of fact, e.g., whether this sheet of paper is white, with very complex matters of right and wrong, e.g., whether the Vietnamese War is right. Take a very simple matter of right or wrong, with no complicating side issues: Is it right to kill someone for no other reason than the fact that you dislike his face? Surely almost any person in almost any age or society would answer that this is not right, but wrong. It is no argument to say that some people would deny this, or would try to justify their own killing of someone for such a trivial reason, for you could find someone to deny any matter of fact you like, especially if the person's own interests were concerned.

If by a question of fact you mean a question which can be decisively settled by using your senses and knowing what words mean, then questions of right or wrong are not questions of fact. But by this standard a great many questions of science or history or politics are not questions of fact either. And unless you can show that every question which is not a question of fact is purely subjective and merely a matter of opinion, then showing that something is not a matter of fact, in some narrow and restricted sense, has no particular sting.

Historically, the idea that moral questions are purely subjective has often been a consequence of more general views. about the nature of facts and the meaning of words. One such view, which has now been rejected by philosophers who have argued out its pros and cons but which is still found among scientists, is the view that any statement that cannot be proved or disproved by the methods of science or mathematics must be purely subjective or emotional. This view has a number of difficulties, but the fatal difficulty is that the view itself cannot be proved (or disproved for that matter) by the methods of science or mathematics. Thus the view is self-destructive if applied to itself. (We can refuse to apply it to itself, but this opens the door to other exceptions and exemptions.)

One thing to note at this point is that those who hold the view that right and wrong are subjective are often inconsistent in applying this principle. Fred, for example, condemned the sexual morality of his home town as "narrow, self-righteous, hypocritical." But by his own principle, if the people in his home town had a feeling of approval toward certain sorts of sexual behavior (and disapproval towards others) then those forms of behavior were right (or wrong) for them. A purely subjective ethics gives no grounds for either condemning or praising anyone else on moral grounds. All you can say is, "I approve of this action and so does he," or "I approve of this action, but she does not."

Does this mean that a subjective attitude towards ethics necessarily leads to tolerance? Not at all. Some people may approve of persecuting people who have different moral attitudes than they have. According to the subjective theory, this means that it is right for them to persecute. When Fred included in his beliefs the idea that "No one could tell anyone else what he ought to do," he was being inconsistent. Obviously people *do* tell others what they ought to do, so what Fred must have meant by "No one *could* . . ." is that no one *ought* to tell others what to do. But according to Fred's own theory this would be just an expression of his attitude, and other people might have other attitudes. Once you have laid down the *general* principle that right and wrong are different for each person, then anything you say after that will be merely an expression of *your* attitudes. Thus anyone who holds the subjective theory is barred from making any further *general* statement about right and wrong. If he says, "Intolerance is wrong," he means only "I disapprove of intolerance."

In this respect the subjective theory is like a sign on a bin of merchandise that says "price as marked." The only thing such a sign tells you about the price of any item is that you must look at the item itself to find the price. The subjective theory says, "Right and wrong depend on the attitudes of each individual." The only thing this tells us about what is right or wrong is that we must examine each individual to find his attitudes. In the "price as marked" bin, knowing the price of one item tells you nothing about the price of any other. In the subjective theory of right and wrong, knowing what one individual feels is right or wrong tells you nothing about what another individual will feel is right or wrong. Once you say "price as marked," all you can do is look at individual prices. Once you have said, "Right or wrong is up to each individual," all you can do is look at individual beliefs.

You might think that it would be possible to have a subjective theory *plus* some built-in limitations (e.g., "tolerate others' moral beliefs"), just as you can have on your bin: "price as marked; nothing over five dollars." But if you consider the arguments by which people try to establish the subjective theory, you can see that this will not work. Most of these arguments depend on the fact of moral disagreement—the fact that two people with the same factual information can disagree on which is right or wrong in a given situation. But of course people disagree about whether it is right to impose one's own moral beliefs on others just as much as they disagree on whether killing or adultery is ever justified. Thus any principle of tolerance is vulnerable to the same arguments by which the subjectivist attacks other moral principles. You cannot consistently use disagreement to argue for subjectivism and then ignore the disagreement about toleration.

The same general difficulties, by the way, arise with theories that try to make right and wrong depend on the attitudes of larger groups of people, say a country or a culture. If what is right in a given country is what the majority of people in that country approve of, then some countries may approve of interfering with what other countries approve and disapprove of. You cannot say, "Right and wrong is what each country (or culture) considers right or wrong" and also consistently object to one country's interfering with the moral ideas of another country. Or rather, you can object (your society approves of objecting), but it is right for the other country to ignore you and interfere (their society approves of interfering). This inconsistency is often found in anthropological writers who maintain that right and wrong vary from culture to culture, but who also want to protest against one culture's imposing its standards on another. But it is quite clear that many empire builders (e.g., the Romans and the British) have had the attitude that it is right to impose their standards on other cultures. And if what is right is what is approved of by a given culture, then it follows that it was right for these empires to impose their standards on others.

In general there is no necessary connection between *relativism* (making right and wrong depend on the attitudes of the individual, the culture, etc.) and tolerance. It often happens, as a matter of fact, that relativists are tolerant of others. But there is no logical reason why a relativist should not say: "Right is what each individual approves of. *I* approve of making you agree with me by any means necessary."

Anthropologists or popularizers of anthropology sometimes talk as if ethical relativism were an integral part of the anthropological methodology. But ethical relativism is a philosophical theory and is no more essential to anthropology than the theories of absolute space and time were essential to Newton's physics. Just as Newton's prestige influenced some physicists to accept absolute space and time, the influence of some notable anthropologists who were ethical relativists has probably caused some anthropologists to accept ethical relativism. But not all anthropologists are ethical relativists and many of them realize that a particular philosophical view about ethics is no more necessary to the practice of anthropology than certain philosophical views about space and time are to the practice of physics. Of course anthropology can supply data which can be used to argue the pros and cons of ethical relativism just as science can give us new information which will affect our philosophical views about space and time. But the Greek philosophers who began the systematic study of ethics were quite aware of considerable variations in codes of conduct in neighboring cultures.

Sometimes anthropologists who favor ethical relativism argue as if the only alternative to relativism were a blind and prejudiced ethnocentrism. But this is merely setting up a straw man to knock down. An anthropologist need not be relativistic about medicine, but can take an open-minded and considerate attitude towards the medical practices of a primitive culture while still maintaining that, e.g., the germ theory of disease is objectively true; similarly, someone who holds an objective ethical theory can still treat moral practices in a primitive culture with respect and consideration.

It may be useful at this point to look at some alternative moral theories. If right and wrong don't depend just on the attitudes of the individual, what do they depend on? We have already looked briefly at one aspect of the theory that they depend on the attitudes of a country or culture. Also, some people hold the theory that right and wrong depend on the attitudes of some divine being or beings. (As we shall see, this is only one possible kind of religious ethics.) This gives us three possible kinds of "attitude" theories:

Right and wrong depend on the attitude of:

A. Each individual human being
B. Groups of human beings
C. Superhuman being or beings

Theory A is what we have been calling *subjectivism*[1] or *individual relativism*. Theory B is what is often called *cultural relativism*, and Theory C is often called the *Divine Will* theory.

As opposed to any of these "attitude" theories, many people hold that right or wrong ought to be determined on the basis of what is "good for" or "beneficial to" individuals or groups of individuals. Thus we can have a theory that is rather like the subjectivist theory except that it says what is right for each individual is what is really beneficial to that individual, not what he approves of. This theory is called *egoism* or *ethical egoism*. It is often very much entangled with another theory called *psychological egoism*, which says that as a matter of fact individuals always *do* act for their own benefit. In the next chapter we will spend some time untangling all of the complications in egoist views of various kinds.

Ethical egoism and subjectivism, though similar, will often give different answers to particular questions of right or wrong. For instance, if a man wished to get drunk every night, subjectivism might say that the action was right for him since he approved of it, but egoism might hold that it was wrong for him since it was damaging his liver and brain

[1] Some writers use "subjectivism" in a wider sense, to refer to any theory which makes right and wrong a matter of personal or group choice.

and thus was not to his real long-term benefit. Again, subjectivism might say that it was right for Harry to rape Sue since he approved of doing it, while egoism might say that it was wrong, since he stood a good chance of being caught and imprisoned. Neither subjectivism nor egoism looks beyond the individual himself for a standard of right or wrong, but they approach the individual differently, subjectivism asking what he approves, egoism asking what will actually benefit him.

Another "benefit" theory is the theory that what is right is what will bring the greatest benefit to the greatest number of persons. Such theories are often called *utilitarian* theories, or *utilitarianism.* When Fred thought of changing his moral principle to "nothing is wrong unless it hurts people," he was moving toward a utilitarian position. In Chapter 3 we will examine some of the pros and cons of utilitarianism.

There is also the possibility of a theory which bases right and wrong on what benefits some superhuman being or beings. But if God or the gods are seen as vastly superior to humans, it is hard to see how human beings could benefit them. This is particularly true of the Judeo-Christian God, who is seen as infinitely superior to man. However, some religious ethics seem to be based on the idea that man can "serve" or "glorify" God or the gods in some way by obeying moral laws laid down by God or the gods. Perhaps a useful analogy here is the way in which we speak of a person "being a credit to" a parent or teacher who is no longer alive to see the good effects of his training.

Thus we have three "benefit" theories.

An action is right if:

A. It is for the greatest good of an individual human being
B. It is for the greatest good of the majority of human beings
C. It is for the greatest good of some superhuman being or beings

Theory A is *ethical egoism*, Theory B is *utilitarianism*, and Theory C we will call the *Divine Glory* theory.

Notice that Theory A in this group, ethical egoism, is like subjectivism and cultural relativism in that an action can be both right and wrong. Thus if X kills Y, a subjectivist might say this was right because X approved, but wrong because Y disapproved. A cultural relativist might say it was right because people in Culture F approved of it but wrong because people in Culture G disapproved of it. An egoist might say it was right because it benefited X but wrong because it did not benefit Y.

In a Divine Will or Divine Glory theory in which there are many gods, the same action may be both right and wrong because it is approved or is to the glory of some gods but not others. In a Divine Will or

Divine Glory theory with only one God, who is consistent and does not change his attitudes or his nature, then presumably a given act will be either definitely right (approved by God or to the glory of God) or definitely wrong. Similarly, in a utilitarian theory an action will either be definitely right (for the greatest good of the greatest number) or definitely wrong. Whether we can always know for sure which actions are which is another story.

Yet another possible basis for determining right and wrong is the nature of persons. If we regard each human being as being so different from every other human being that the differences are morally significant, we get yet another kind of individualistic ethics. This involves saying that what is right for Peter may be wrong for Paul, not because of any general characteristics of the situation (e.g., Peter married and Paul not; Paul a child, Peter an adult, etc.), but just because Peter is Peter and Paul is Paul. According to this theory, which we will call *ethical individualism*, there is no "human nature" such that what is right for one man is right for every other man in the same circumstances. Since each individual is unique, each action and each set of circumstances are unique. This theory is sometimes called *situation ethics* and we will look at it more closely in Chapter 5.

A more traditional kind of theory bases right and wrong on a human nature that is common to all human beings, or perhaps on a "rational nature" common to any possible rational being. I will call this theory the *human nature* theory of ethics. For any human nature theory of ethics the question "What is man?" is of vital importance, and you will get importantly different views of what is right or wrong from different views of human nature. If man is only an animal, one moral view seems appropriate; if man is a soul imprisoned in a body, another, and so on.

Not always clearly distinguished from human nature theories of ethics are those theories that base right and wrong on the nature of God or on the nature of some impersonal "moral law." I will call this theory the *natural law* theory of ethics. It was held by the Stoic philosophers in ancient times, and has been held by many Christian philosophers and theologians, both Protestant and Catholic. It has some claim to being the main Christian ethical theory, although the simple Divine Will theory is often attacked as the only kind of "religious" ethics.

If we were going to discuss in any adequate way the justifiability of the human nature or natural law theories of ethics, it would be necessary to say a great deal about metaphysics and philosophy of religion. But since both human nature and natural law theories agree that we can give moral rules which apply to all human beings, we can consider this aspect of those theories without getting too far afield. Thus, rather than consider human nature or natural law theories separately, in Chapter 4 we will discuss the advantages and disadvantages of any theory which claims that morality is founded on ethical rules.

We thus have nine general kinds of ethical theory, arranged under three headings:

I. Attitude Theories
   A. Subjectivism
   B. Cultural Relativism
   C. Divine Will Theory

II. Benefit Theories
   A. Ethical Egoism
   B. Utilitarianism
   C. Divine Glory Theory

III. Nature Theories
   A. Individualism
   B. Human Nature Theory
   C. Natural Law Theory

Notice that all of the A theories are based on the individual, all of the B theories are based on society or humanity as a whole, and all of the C theories are religious or at least bring in some realm of values outside individuals or groups of individuals.

This is one possible division of theories; there could be many other arrangements, using other principles of classification. There is another quite different way of dividing the subject matter of ethics. This division depends on the source of our knowledge about ethics. One philosophical position is that we have no knowledge of right and wrong; this position is called *noncognitivism.* Another position is that we can know whether a thing is right or wrong by simply looking at factual information; this position is called *naturalism.* A third position holds that we need something more than factual information to know whether a thing is right or wrong; this position we will call *non-naturalism.* A particularly important sort of non-naturalism is the view that we have some sort of direct insight into the rightness or wrongness of particular actions or into the truth of moral rules. This view is called *intuitionism.*

Noncognitivism rejects all of the moral theories we have considered, insofar as they claim to know something definite about right and wrong (though a noncognitivist might *choose* or *prefer* one of these theories). But in practice people often confuse noncognitivism with subjectivism or cultural relativism. Theoretically, each of the nine theories we considered could have a naturalistic and a non-naturalistic version. As a matter of history, however, utilitarian theories have usually been naturalistic, and natural law theories non-naturalistic. The other theories, as we shall see, occur in both naturalistic and non-naturalistic versions.

Yet another division which is often made in ethical theories is the distinction between *teleological* theories, which determine right or wrong by looking at the *consequences* of actions, and *deontological* theories, which look at the *nature* of the action as well as its consequences. Deontological theories tend to take the view that there are some actions which are wrong regardless of consequences, while teleological theories tend to deny this. Attitude theories would have to be classed as deontological because what makes an act right or wrong on an attitude theory is not its consequences, but whether or not the act is approved. Benefit theories, especially utilitarianism, tend to be teleological, whereas nature theories tend to be deontological since the nature of persons, of God, or of a moral law is what determines right or wrong, and not consequences. The difference in practice between teleological and deontological theories can often be very small if the teleological theory in question interprets "consequences" very broadly, and if the deontological theory takes consequences into account as one of the factors in judging the action.

When we examine an ethical theory it can often be very illuminating to ask: "What information would we need in order to know what things are right and wrong if this theory is true?" or "Are consequences the only thing to be considered on this theory?" But in general, classifications like "naturalistic/non-naturalistic" or "teleological/deontological" are not especially useful for people who are in moral perplexities like Fred's. It is more useful to start with concrete theories of ethics which have been held by large groups of people and have actually been used to guide conduct. In the next four chapters of this book, this is the procedure we will follow. Then, having gotten some idea of the main ethical theories, in the final five chapters we will look at some of the moral problems that face us, and see how the various theories would deal with these problems.

DISCUSSION QUESTIONS

Discuss the following defenses of subjectivism:

1. If you don't agree that right is what you believe is right, then you must think that right is what someone else believes is right. And why should you be guided by what someone else thinks is right?

2. Any objectively true view can be justified by observation or calculation. Moral views cannot be justified by observation or calculation, so they must be subjective.
3. If ethics were objective, as science is, then there would be general agreement about ethical truths, just as there is general agreement about scientific truths. But look how people disagree about, for example, the ethical justifiability of abortion, or war, or capital punishment. Ethics is obviously just a matter of individual opinion.

Discuss the following criticisms of subjectivism:

4. If subjectivism were true there would be no such thing as ethical argument, just as there is no real argument about matters of taste. But people do give reasonable arguments in ethics, convince each other, arrive at general agreement. So subjectivism must be false.
5. If subjectivism were true, we couldn't give moral advice to others any more than I can advise you what to eat or who to date on the basis of my own likes or dislikes. But people do seek and give and accept moral advice; so subjectivism must be false.

Discuss the following arguments pro and con for cultural relativism and the Divine Will theory.

6. People in the United States regard racial discrimination as wrong, but people in Rhodesia and South Africa regard it as right; so we have no right to interfere with racial discrimination in those countries.
7. Since there is nothing at all which has not been regarded as right by some culture and wrong by some other cultures, if cultural relativism were true we could make no absolute moral judgments. But some things, for instance torturing innocent children merely for your own pleasure, are absolutely wrong. Thus cultural relativism cannot be true.
8. If the only standard of right and wrong were the will of God, then God could decide tomorrow that justice and kindness were wrong and injustice and cruelty were right. This is absurd, so there must be some other standard.
9. If God did create man, then God surely would have the right to lay down standards for man's behavior. Thus if you believe in a Creator, you will naturally accept a Divine Will theory of ethics.

Write a brief essay on the following question:

10. Was Fred right or wrong in attacking Harry? What should he have done?

FURTHER READINGS

Ewing, A. C., *Ethics*, pp. 9-20. New York: The Free Press, 1953.

Frankena, William, *Ethics* (2nd ed.), pp. 1-16. Englewood Cliffs, N.J.: Prentice-Hall, Inc., 1973.

Frankena, William, and John Granrose, *Introductory Readings in Ethics*. Englewood Cliffs, N.J.: Prentice-Hall, Inc., 1974:

Broad, C. D., "Ought We to Fight for Our Country," pp. 29-37.

Dewey, John, "Reflective Morality and Ethical Theory," pp. 13-17.

Lemmon, John, "Moral Dilemmas," pp. 17-28.

Plato, *Crito* (selections), pp. 3-10; *Protagoras* (selections), pp. 10-12.

Sellars, Wilfred, and John Hospers, *Readings in Ethical Theory* (2nd ed.). New York: Appleton-Century-Crofts, 1970:

Ayer, A. J., "Critique of Ethics," pp. 422-429.

Ross, W. D., "Critique of Ayer," pp. 250-252.

Stevenson, C. L., "The Emotive Meaning of Ethical Terms," pp. 254-266.

———, "The Emotive Conception of Ethics and Its Cognitive Implications, pp. 267-275.

Wellman, Carl, "Emotivism and Ethical Objectivity," pp. 276-287.

2 *Egoism: Is It Human To Be Selfish?*

When Sam Shapiro left college with a degree in Communications, he had all kinds of hopes and ambitions. So he was somewhat bemused to find himself a year later working as a salesman for a big roofing contractor—the only job he had been able to get. Not that Sam was doing badly in financial terms; it even looked as if he and his girlfriend Becca might be able to afford to get married soon. And he found himself, rather unexpectedly, enjoying selling. His company had a good product and he felt that he was being of real service to his customers. But it was this attitude of wanting to be of service that eventually got Sam into trouble with the sales manager, Frank Smith.

When Smith called Sam into his office one day for "a little talk," Sam knew that this meant trouble. But he wasn't sure why. His sales record was as good as most of the salesmen's, though not as good as some of those who used every trick and device to make a sale. It turned out that this was the trouble. "Sam, I like you," said Smith. "I think you have the ability to be a really great salesman, and someday to sit where I'm sitting. But if that's what you want you've got to bear down. Now what's this I hear about your tearing up a signed contract last month?"

"I can explain that," replied Sam. "Old Mrs. McIlhaney just couldn't afford the payments on her pension money. She'd been counting on her married daughter to help a little each month, but the daughter couldn't or wouldn't. It was no use getting started on the job if she couldn't pay."

Smith leaned back in his swivel chair and looked at Sam. "Didn't it occur to you that we'd have a lien on her house and that if she didn't pay we'd be able to force a sale and maybe get the house? That's a nice little bit of property, Sam."

Sam flushed and started to say something, but controlled himself with an effort. "No, sir, it didn't occur to me," was all he said.

"And another thing, Shapiro, what's this I hear about your recommendiing another company to one of your prospects?" went on Smith in a less friendly tone.

Sam didn't sound apologetic this time. "We just didn't have the right materials for that roof in our line, Mr. Smith. We couldn't have done a good job and there would have been a lot of ill will on the part of the customer."

Frank Smith looked at Sam, exasperation on his face. "Shapiro, what the hell do you think you're selling, cars? A good roof will last forty, fifty years in this climate. You'd have a long grey beard before you got repeat business. The trouble with you, Shapiro, is that you're forgetting that you've got to look after number one. Nobody's going to take care of your interests if *you* don't. Let the customers look after themselves. Your job is to *sell*, not to hold the customers' hands and make sure they don't waste their money. I thought you people were supposed to be good businessmen."

Sam hardly noticed the ethnic slur, he was so angry about the rest of what Smith had said. "Mr. Smith, I couldn't disagree with you more. As a matter of fact I think it *is* good business to think about your customers' interests and do the best job you can for them. But even if it wasn't, I wouldn't step on everybody's face just to make myself a few extra bucks. There's more to living in this world than just getting everything you can for yourself."

"Don't kid yourself," Smith sneered. "Everyone is out for what they can get. If you want to get your kicks being a social worker, fine. But that's just your way of feeling important. Nobody does anything unless there's something in it for them."

Sam looked at him. "Mr. Smith, you don't even live up to that yourself. I don't like your business methods but I do admire the way you've stuck to your wife through this long illness. One

> reason you're so touchy, I know, is all the extra work you do to make her comfortable. And I know some of the girls in the office would be happy to 'console' you for what you're missing at home. I admire the way you've turned them down."
>
> Smith was red in the face. "You keep my private life out of this, Shapiro. I couldn't live with myself if I let down my wife after all we've been through together, but that's none of your business."
>
> Sam stood up. "I didn't say it was, Mr. Smith. I'm only saying that you don't act as cynically as you talk. I'm going to take a chance on that, because I'm going to keep on trying to be honest and helpful to my customers. If you want to fire me for that, go ahead."
>
> Smith swiveled his chair to look out the window. "Oh, get out of here, Shapiro, nobody said anything about firing you. I said what I did for your own good."
>
> Sam opened the door, then turned to Smith. "Thanks for trying to help me, Mr. Smith. But how do you square *that* with what you've said about only looking out for number one?" And Sam went out, closing the door softly behind him.

The point of view expressed by Frank Smith is one we frequently hear. It is often not clear whether someone like Smith is claiming that each person *does as a matter of fact* act only in his own interests or whether he is saying that each person *should* act only in his own interests. The first view is called *psychological egoism*, the second view is called *ethical egoism*.

Psychological egoism, the view that each person does as a matter of fact act only in his own interests, is a popular view but one which will not stand up to careful examination. Usually its defenders take it as obvious that each person acts in the way which he thinks will make him happy. If someone points out obvious cases of altruism or self-sacrifice, the psychological egoist tries to explain these away as attempts to gain some other kind of gratification—just as Frank Smith tried to explain Sam's concern for his customers as a desire to feel important. In cases where there seems to be no positive source of gratification they argue that the person doing the apparently self-sacrificing or altruistic action is trying to avoid some unpleasant feeling or experience. Frank Smith, remember, said he "couldn't live with himself" if he was unfaithful to his wife. Thus the complete psychological egoist theory would hold that "each person always acts in the way which he thinks will gain some form of happiness for himself or avoid some form of unhappiness for himself."

This sounds convincing because of the ambiguity of words like "happiness" and "unhappiness." There are three main things which might be meant by "happiness." The first is joy or delight, "getting a kick out of it." The corresponding sense of unhappiness is feeling mental or physical pain, being sad, gloomy, disgusted, "down." But it is quite obvious as a matter of experience that people do do a great many things which do *not* bring them joy and delight and which *do* bring them mental or physical pain. So if "happiness" and "unhappiness" mean "joy" and "pain," the psychological egoist theory is false as a matter of common experience; people do not always act so as to gain joy or avoid pain.

"Happiness" can also mean "satisfaction, tranquility, peace of mind." The corresponding sense of "unhappiness" is "dissatisfaction, worry, uneasiness." But it is also quite clear as a matter of experience that people do not always act in such a way as to gain satisfaction or tranquility or to avoid dissatisfaction or worry. Of course in some cases we "trade off" worry or dissatisfaction for joy or pleasure, but in many cases we act in ways which are neither delightful nor satisfying.

The final sense of "happiness" is "getting what you want," "getting your own way," and the corresponding sense of "unhappiness" is "being frustrated," "not achieving your desires." If by this kind of happiness we mean "getting what we would really like," or "getting what we would prefer," then obviously a good many things we do do not gain us happiness in this sense, and do lead to frustration. If we try to make this sense of happiness "making what seems to be the best choice available in the circumstances," then it is probably true that people *almost* always make what seems to them the best choice available in the circumstances. (Not always, because sometimes in anger, perversity, or whim, we make just any old choice.) But this doesn't mean that we get what we like *or* like what we get.

But when we stretch the idea of happiness this far, all that we are saying is that people choose what they choose, or that they almost always try to make the best choice available in the circumstances. But the term "best choice available" is ambiguous. In certain circumstances many people choose actions that bring them no joy or satisfaction—actions which are not what they really want or prefer. In many cases these actions seem to them the "best" because they would benefit someone else, or because they believe that these actions are morally right.

Thus the principle that "each person always acts in the way which he thinks will gain some form of happiness for himself or avoid some form of unhappiness for himself" is just false as a matter of experience if we take happiness in the sense of "joy," or "satisfaction," or "getting what you want" in a strong sense. Only if we take "happiness" in the weak sense of "making what seems to you to be the best choice available in the circumstances" is psychological egoism even fairly plausible. If all this means is that "you choose what you choose," it is true but perfectly empty and trivial. If we try to make it even a little stronger, e.g., "you choose what in the circumstances is in some sense best for *yourself*," it turns out to be false as a matter of experience. Some people act all of the time and most people act some of the time for motives that are not purely self-interested.

To remind ourselves of the great variety of human motives for action, let us try a sort of schematic diagram. We will use the small letters *g* and *b* to mean "good for oneself" and "bad for oneself," and the capital letters G and *B* to mean "good for others" and "bad for others." When we write two of these letters with an arrow between them we will read this as "Doing something which is __________ in order to bring about __________." For example,

$$g \rightarrow G$$

should be read as "Doing something which is good for ourselves in order to bring about good for others." There are eight cases which we can distinguish in this way:

1. g → G

   (Doing something good for oneself in order to bring about good for others)

   Example: Someone who enjoys singing sings for old people at a Christmas party at a rest home in order to help them enjoy the holiday. We might call this decent behavior.

2. b → G

   (Doing something bad for oneself in order to bring about good for others)

   Example: A friend of the singer who has no special talent and dislikes washing dishes washes dishes after the Christmas party so that the rest home staff can have a holiday. We can call this altruistic behavior.

3. g → B

   (Doing something good for oneself in order to bring about bad for others)

   Example: The singer practices some of her favorite songs late at night with the window open in order to annoy a grouchy neighbor. We will call this malicious behavior.

4. b → B

   (Doing something bad for oneself in order to bring about bad for others)

Example: The grouchy neighbor gets out of bed and stands in his cold garage in his pajamas running his power mower in order to get back at the singer. We will call this spiteful behavior.

5. G → g
   (Doing something good for others in order to bring about good for oneself)

Example: The singer gives a concert which is enjoyed by the audience, but her only motive is her own enjoyment and the concert fee. We can call this self-serving behavior.

6. B → g
   (Doing something bad for others in order to bring about good for oneself)

Example: The singer's manager steals the box-office receipts and flies off for a luxurious vacation in Europe. We will call this selfish behavior.

7. G → b
   (Doing something good for others in order to bring about bad for oneself)

Example: The singer's ex-boyfriend takes the singer and her new husband out to dinner, knowing it will make him feel terrible to see their happiness. We will call this self-torturing behavior.

8. B → b
   (Doing something bad for others in order to bring about bad for oneself)

Example: The singer's manager continues to steal from others, knowing he will soon be caught and imprisoned. We will call this self-destructive behavior.

To summarize:

1.	g	→	G	Decent behavior
2.	b	→	G	Altruistic behavior
3.	g	→	B	Malicious behavior
4.	b	→	B	Spiteful behavior
5.	G	→	g	Self-serving behavior
6.	B	→	g	Selfish behavior
7.	G	→	b	Self-torturing behavior
8.	B	→	b	Self-destructive behavior

Now of course this list is somewhat artificial and highly simplified,* but

* It ignores cases such as g→g, B→B, etc. as well as complex cases such as g→(g *and* G) But our purpose here is not a complete characterization of motives.

it can be useful for certain purposes. In the first place all of these kinds of behavior do occur. All of us have probably engaged in all of these kinds of behavior at one time or another. We could find examples of all of them in literature or for that matter in the daily newspapers. Extreme cases of self-torturing or self-destructive behavior may be rare and often indicate psychological disturbances, but less dramatic instances are fairly common.

A strict psychological egoist would have to deny that any of these kinds of behavior occur except for selfish and self-serving behavior. A more liberal psychological egoist might admit that decent behavior and malicious behavior sometimes occurred. But any kind of psychological egoist would presumably have to deny that altruistic, spiteful, self-torturing, or self-destructive behavior occurs. Yet it is a familiar and obvious fact that all of these kinds of behavior do occur.

There are two possible objections to the view that people sometimes act unselfishly. First, someone might claim that it is false as a matter of fact, that everyone does act from selfish motives in a straightforward sense. Apparent examples to the contrary are just cases of hypocrisy or hidden motives. People who maintain such a position are sometimes those who have been unfortunate enough never to have known a really unselfish person, or perhaps have known too well a hypocrite who pretended to unselfishness. Only wider experience would really convince anyone who favored psychological egoism for such reasons. In other cases people defend ethical egoism because they themselves are selfish and cannot imagine anyone acting from unselfish motives. Such people present a practical or ethical problem rather than a logical one.

But the second objection to this view is really a logical one, and conceals a logical fallacy. This objection rests on the idea that if anyone chooses to act in a certain way it *must* "pay off" for him in some way. Otherwise, it is said, why would he choose to act in that way? If we look hard enough, we will find a self-interested motive. But we can reply to such an objection that it simply assumes what it is trying to prove. In many cases we can look as long and carefully as we like and not discover anything that would ordinarily be called a selfish motive for an action. If the psychological egoist continues to insist that there *must* be a selfish motive, we will suspect that he has made up his mind in advance that all actions are selfish and that what he means by "looking hard enough" is looking until we do find a selfish motive. But of course it is then true by definition that if we haven't found a selfish motive we haven't looked hard enough (that is, looked until we found a selfish motive).

In fact there is a more general philosophical error behind this version of psychological egoism. If we take an unbiased look at motives for action, we find that people act for various motives: to please themselves, to please others, to live up to a moral code or ideal. The psychological egoist ignores all but one of these motives and says that we always act to please ourselves. This is either factually false or it is made emptily true by stretching the idea of "pleasing ourselves" to cover *any* voluntary action, no matter what the motive. This psychological egoism is either factually false or it is a logical trick.

Ethical egoism is often confused with psychological egoism, but is quite different. Psychological egoism makes the factual claim that everyone *does* act only in their own interest. Ethical egoism says that people *ought* to act only in their own interest, and usually goes on to say that people who do not are foolish or deluded. There is an immediate problem here, for what does the ethical egoist mean by "ought"? Sometimes we use "ought" in a *hypothetical* way, as when we say, "*If* you want to get to Sydney as quickly as possible, you ought to fly Qantas." But of course if you don't want to get to Sydney, the "ought" does not apply. Now if the "ought" in ethical egoism is a hypothetical "ought," what is ethical egoism saying? If it is merely saying, "If you want to serve only your own interests you ought to act only in your own interests," then it would be trivial and empty.

Some ethical egoists seem to be making the factual claim, "If you want to be happy, then you ought to act only in your own interests." But as a factual claim this would seem to be false. Many selfish people are quite unhappy, and many unselfish people are very happy. Thus, acting only in your own interests is neither sufficient nor necessary for happiness.

One variant of ethical egoism that is sometimes defended is the idea that if each person looks after his own interests exclusively this will somehow work out as best for everyone. This is odd in two ways. First it seems to aim at the benefit of everyone as an end, making selfishness only a means. Thus perhaps it should not be classified as an egoist theory at all, but rather as a kind of utilitarianism. The other odd thing is that anyone could seriously believe that everyone could be benefited by general selfishness. Fairly obviously, those with power, talent, etc. would advance their own interests much more effectively than those without, bringing about unhappiness, frustration, and want among the "have-nots." Whatever attractiveness this theory may have is probably due to the fact that it serves as a comfortable rationalization for the more fortunate. They can act selfishly and yet feel that they are serving the general good.

Some theories that sound egoistic actually are not. For example, some Greek philosophers held that a man should do what is best for himself, but maintained that what *is* best for any man is virtue. By "virtue" they meant acting justly, benevolently, etc., just the sort of behavior that ordinary ethical egoism rejects as foolish. Thus these Greek philosophers used what sounds like egoistic arguments to recommend unselfishness and self-sacrifice. Socrates accepted a death sentence rather than agree to stop his efforts to make his fellow countrymen face up to problems of truth and morality. But he argued that this choice was only reasonable, for it would be far worse for him to become evil (by abandoning his duty out of fear) than it would be for him to be killed. Some Christian writers speak of a man's first duty as saving his own soul. This sounds selfish, but when we ask them how a man is to save his soul the answer is, "by unselfish love of God and our fellow men." Thus again, what at first sounds like egoism turns out to be opposed to egoism in the usual sense. (Of course there is much more to say both about Socrates' theory and about Christian theories of ethics; they are mentioned here only because of the apparently egoistic element in them.)

Sometimes an ethical egoist will seize on the apparent egoism in a particular view and say, for instance, "The Greek philosophers were concerned only with their own excellence, and the Christians were really egoists." But when we look more closely we find, as we have seen, that both these groups recommend self-sacrifice for the good of others, which is contrary to egoism in the ordinary sense. Thus they are not allies, but opponents of the egoist.

We have seen that if the ethical egoist's "ought" is a hypothetical "ought," then it either becomes empty or involves factually false assumptions or else leads to a theory that is not, after all, egoistic. Suppose, however, that the "ought" in "everyone ought to act only in their own interests" is interpreted not as a hypothetical "ought" but as a nonhypothetical, or *categorical* "ought" of the kind that seems to be characteristic of moral or ethical statements: "No matter what your own desires, you ought morally to act only in your own interests."

Actually very few ethical egoists hold anything like this theory in its pure form. Most popular ethical egoists—Ayn Rand, for example—mix up different varieties of justification, sometimes promising individual joy as the result of egoism, sometimes using the "best for everyone" justification, sometimes using what sounds like a categorical or moral "ought." But suppose someone does try to maintain that we ought, in some categorical or moral sense, to act only in our own interests? How can they back up this claim?

This leads us to the general problem of how to back up *any* claim that we "ought" to do something in the moral, nonhypothetical sense of "ought." The most frequent way is to appeal to some sort of direct moral insight or intuition—the view we call "intuitionism" in Chapter 1. The great stumbling block of such arguments is the fact of moral disagreement. As we shall see, the intuitionist has some replies to this argument, which depend on appealing to the essential agreement of all moral codes at all times and places. But the ethical egoist cannot make such a reply, for only a very few people have ever claimed to have an insight or intuition that selfishness is right; not even all ethical egoists make such a claim. Thus if the ethical egoist claims an intuition or insight, it is one which the overwhelming majority of people have never had. And it is hard to see how the egoist could convince anyone that his intuition was correct.

If the ethical egoist appeals to facts rather than moral intuition, it does his case little good. He would have to claim that some fact or set of facts shows that we ought to serve only our own interests. But what fact or set of facts could show this? It is at this point that many ethical egoists fall back on psychological egoism. But aside from the fact that ethical egoism will not stand up to argument, this is a curious retreat. For if psychological egoism is true, we cannot help serving only our own interests. What then is the point of saying that we *ought* to serve only our own interests?

In the face of such arguments as these, ethical egoists sometimes retreat to a position which amounts to a sort of noncognitivism or ethical skepticism. Their position is, in essence: "I am determined to act only in my own interests, and no argument you can give will convince me that I ought to do otherwise." Of course, in a way this is not an ethical theory at all, but only the announcement of a decision or determination. The sting, however, lies in the implication that there are no good arguments that could convince someone that he ought not to be selfish. Is this true or not?

It is true in this sense: If someone refuses to admit any motives for action except personal advantage, then he cannot be convinced that he ought to do anything that is not to his personal advantage. But similarly, if a skeptic refuses to accept any evidence except this own immediate experience, he cannot be convinced of anything beyond his own immediate experience. If a skeptic refuses to admit any arguments except deductive arguments, he cannot be convinced of the truth of anything that cannot be proved deductively. If a fundamental skeptic refuses to accept any evidence or any argument, he cannot be convinced of anything. The point is not whether a skeptic can reject any particular kind of evidence or argument—obviously he is free to do so. The point is whether such a rejection is reasonable.

Each kind of skepticism must be met on its own ground. Every kind of skeptic except the fundamental skeptic admits some kind of evidence or argument. Why does he accept these but not others? How does he justify accepting some of the things that other men regard as reasonable, and rejecting others. For it is quite clear that we ordinarily do admit arguments which are not deductive, accept evidence other than the evidence of our immediate experience, and so on. In ethics we do take it as reasonable to act in order to benefit others or to live up to a moral code. The ethical egoist must give some reason for rejecting the benefit of others or living up to a moral code as reasons for action while accepting his own advantage as a reason for action. And it would seem that he cannot do this. He can, of course, simply reject these reasons for action without giving any reasons for the rejection. But an unreasoned rejection seems unreasonable, and has no power to change our convictions as to what is reasonable. You do not refute or even cast doubt on a position or an argument by simply refusing to accept it for no reason.

This question of ethical skepticism is one which we will return to at the end of the book. But for the moment we can say that we have strong arguments against both psychological egoism and ethical egoism and no good arguments in favor of either view.

DISCUSSION QUESTIONS

1. People in love often seem to behave unselfishly. How would a psychological egoist explain this? Would this explanation be convincing to you?
2. People who hate others sometimes ruin themselves trying to hurt their enemies. Is this a problem for the egoist? Why or why not?
3. What other meanings can you find for "happiness" than the three discussed in the chapter? Would any of these other meanings affect the question of egoism?
4. Does economic theory lend support to psychological egoism? To ethical egoism? Why or why not?
5. How would you convince a cynical person that people do in fact sometimes act unselfishly?
6. From what motives do you generally act? Egoistic? Altruistic? A mixture? How typical do you think you are?
7. Does selfishness lead to happiness? Why or why not?
8. Look at some argument for ethical egoism—for example, in one of Ayn Rand's books. What arguments are given? How strong are they?
9. Make the strongest case you can for or against ethical egoism. How might an opponent reply to you?
10. Defend either Frank Smith's or Sam Shapiro's point of view, using the imagined facts in the story as the basis of your defense.

FURTHER READINGS

Ewing, A. C., *Ethics*, pp. 21-35. New York: The Free Press, 1953.

Frankena, William, *Ethics* (2nd ed.), pp. 17-22. Englewood Cliffs, N.J.: Prentice-Hall, Inc., 1973.

Frankena, William, and John Granrose, *Introductory Readings in Ethics.* Englewood Cliffs, N.J.: Prentice-Hall, Inc., 1974.

Butler, Joseph, "A 'Refutation' of Egoism," pp. 49-58.

Cicero, "The Ethics of Epicurus: Egoism," pp. 42-49.

Ewing, A. C., "Against Ethical Egoism," pp. 58-61.

Hospers, John, "Baier and Medlin on Ethical Egoism," pp. 61-67.

Rand, Ayn, *The Virtue of Selfishness.* New York: New American Library, 1964.

Sellars, Wilfred, and John Hospers, *Readings in Ethical Theory* (2nd ed.). New York: Appleton-Century-Crofts, 1970:

Broad, C. D., "Remarks on Psychological Hedonism," pp. 686-689.

Hospers, John, "Why Be Moral?" pp. 730-737.

Prichard, H. A., "Duty and Interest," pp. 690-703.

3 *Utilitarianism: The Greatest Good . . .*

There was once a student prince named Peter. While he was at college, Prince Peter read the works of the great English utilitarian, John Stuart Mill, and became completely convinced that the right thing to do was always the action which would bring the greatest good to the greatest number of people. Peter was a conscientious, but rather dull young man, who had always wanted to do the right thing, and now he was sure he had found a perfect formula for doing it. He set to work enthusiastically to put his newfound principle into action.

But oddly enough, Peter's friends found that his actions seemed to change for the worse in some ways. Before he had discovered John Stuart Mill, Peter had been a very reliable person. You could always trust him to keep his word, to pay his debts, to repay kindnesses done him. But now he began to break promises to his friends, and when reproached he explained gravely that, after calculating, he had concluded that more good would be done by breaking his promise.

Prince Peter of course received a generous allowance, but money ran through his fingers easily. His friend Dick had loaned him money several times and had always been repaid when Peter's money arrived from home. But on the next occasion Dick was not repaid. The beggars to whom Peter gave the money were very happy, but Dick had loaned Peter far more than he could afford to lose, counting on his friend's word. Peter's other friends tried to reason with him, but he always seemed to have something to do which by his calculations would cause greater good than talking with his friends. And of course he was right, by his principles, for there is a good deal of unhappiness in the world, and a man who seriously tries to rule his every action by the principle of the greatest good for the greatest number will find himself very busy indeed.

Perhaps left to private life and to the persuasions of his friends Peter might have modified his views in time but, unfortunately, just at this time old King Paul died and Peter became King. Peter's kingdom was a small one, but very old-fashioned, and in it Peter was an absolute monarch. Still on fire with his new principle, Peter began to issue edicts soon after his coronation. The people were shocked when Peter moved his mother out of the palace to an old people's home, even though Peter pointed out all the good he could do for the poor with the money it had cost to maintain the old Queen. But it was not until Peter began his executions that people began to think of revolt.

Peter had the best intentions, of course. He carefully explained to the people that there were two ways of increasing the sum total of happiness: by adding happiness and by subtracting unhappiness. By his immediate execution of all people suffering from painful and incurable diseases Peter calculated that he had increased the net happiness in his kingdom considerably. He admitted that he had caused unhappiness to some of the relatives of those executed, but they would get over it. It was not a matter of expense, Peter explained, even though many of the medical resources of the kingdom were now freed to make the people healthier. In the insane asylums, for instance, Peter had killed only those suffering from melancholy, sparing all those whose insanity seemed to leave them happy.

The last straw, however, was probably the Happiness Committees which Peter proposed. These committees were to hear complaints against citizens who were alleged to cause more unhappiness than happiness by their existence, and were empowered to summarily execute those whose unhappiness-causing qualities could not be altered. When one of the committees ordered the execution of a gentle young man with a harelip and a deformed body, on the

> grounds that looking at him caused unhappiness to many people, this was the last straw. Grand Duke Edmund, Peter's cousin, led the successful revolt. At the head of his troops he stormed the palace, and as Edmund plunged his sword into Peter's heart he cried: "Sorry, cousin! But *this*, at any rate, is for the greatest good of the greatest number!"

What was the cause of Peter's troubles? He was a conscientious man, and his principle, "The greatest good of the greatest number," is one that seems to many people to be reasonable. Why, then, did Peter become a bad friend, a bad son, a cruel executioner? One possible answer is that Peter had too narrow an idea of good. He seemed to consider only happiness as good, and perhaps this was his mistake.

The idea that happiness or pleasure is the only good that needs to be considered is called *hedonism*, and the combination of this with a "greatest happiness" principle would be *hedonistic utilitarianism*. It would seem that this view is open to serious objections. If pleasure or happiness is the only good, then everything else—knowledge, love, beauty, fairness—is only as good as a means to pleasure or happiness. If this were true then a situation in which there was a higher degree of total happiness or pleasure would always be better than one in which there was even a slightly lower degree, even if the situation containing the lower degree of happiness contained all sorts of other good things—love, intelligence, beauty, etc., and the situation containing the higher degree contained none of these things.

For instance, imagine two situations involving the same group of people. In situation 1, these people spend much of their time lying around stoned on some drug which gives them a highly euphoric sensation. In situation 2, the same people are slightly less happy, but their happiness arises from love between members of the group, from knowledge and appreciation of the world around them, and so on. We could imagine that the first group was totally dominated by some tyrant who kept them in line by controlling their supply of the drug (Aldous Huxley's novel *Brave New World* pictures a civilization rather like this). The second group, let us imagine, makes up its mind about what to do by a process of free and democratic discussion. Now the hedonistic utilitarian would have to say that situation 1 was better than situation 2, simply because there was slightly more total happiness in that situation. This conclusion seems to reduce hedonistic utilitarianism to absurdity.

In response to this criticism a utilitarian might reply that he need not be a hedonist. He might argue that utilitarianism can be restated in such a way that the "greatest good" includes all sorts of good things besides happiness or pleasure. Perhaps there is no single thing which is *the* good. Perhaps we can always make a good situation better by adding not only more of the kinds of good already present, but also by adding other kinds of good. The "greatest good," then, will be arrived at by considering goods of *all* kinds. This view is what is often called *ideal utilitarianism.* An ideal utilitarian would argue that it is not the "greatest good" principle that is at fault, but the confusion of the greatest good with pleasure or happiness.

Let us consider, however, what differences this would make in the case of Peter. Suppose that we grant that friendship, for example, is good in itself, apart from any pleasure or happiness it might cause. Even so, the claims of friendship would have to be weighed against other goods, and Peter might end up acting in just the same way, if other goods outweighed the good of friendship. Peter's friends still could not count on him, for in any given instance Peter might decide that the "greatest good" consisted in doing something other than what he had promised. Similarly, even if Peter granted that family affection was a good, he might still send his mother to the old people's home on the grounds that he could do more good to others in this way. Similarly, he might execute innocent people not necessarily because they were unhappy or caused unhappiness, but because they were friendless, or unable to learn, or unable to appreciate beauty. Any kind of theory that tries to calculate the greatest possible good, and then do the action which will bring the greatest good, seems open to the "elimination argument." In other words, make things better by eliminating evil, which in practice may mean killing innocent people because they are unhappy or loveless or defective in some way.

In general, any kind of "greatest good" theory seems to be open to objections along these lines. The action which brings the greatest good to the greatest number of people may bring unjustified harm to a minority, or it may involve breaking some commitment. And it seems there must be something wrong with an ethical theory that tells us to harm innocent people or break our commitments, not as the lesser evil (that might be justifiable) but just in order to benefit other people.

One way of trying to avoid such objections to make a distinction between *act utilitarianism* and *rule utilitarianism.* Theories that say that for each particular act we should calculate the consequences and do what brings the greatest good are called *act utilitarian* theories. *Rule utilitarianism* differs from act utilitarianism in that one decides whether particular actions are right or wrong according to moral rules, and justifies the rules themselves in terms of which rule will bring the greatest good if adopted. A rule utilitarian might argue, for example, that Peter should not have put his mother in an old people's home because this violated a moral rule which tells us to love and take care of our families. This rule in turn is justified by the fact that much more good is done by having such a rule than by not having it. Act utilitarianism may consider only pleasure or happiness as good, in which case it is *hedonistic act utilitarianism,* or it may consider that there are a variety of goods, in which case it is called *ideal act utilitarianism.* Rule utilitarianism also may be either hedonistic or ideal.

There seems to be a good deal to be said for the distinction between act and rule utilitarianism. There are two quite different sorts of questions. One type of question has the general form: "What *kind* of rule (if any) should we have to cover this situation?" The second type of question is: "Have the rules agreed on or passed by the proper authority, been *kept*?" We might, for example, ask what regulations we should have to cover snowmobiles, or noise pollution, or long hair. In some cases (e.g., long hair) we may decide that no rules are necessary. In other cases we may decide that it is in everyone's interest to have certain recognized regulations. Apartment dwellers may make an informal agreement about keeping noise down after a certain hour in the evening; a campsite may have posted regulations forbidding noisy activities between certain hours; a city may have laws against certain sorts of noise. It might be argued that it is only the rules themselves that are decided on the basis of the "greatest good of the greatest number," and that once appropriate rules have been passed we should either keep the rules or have the rules changed by some appropriate process. We need not and, indeed, should not appeal directly to the greatest good of the greatest number in judging particular actions. The right questions to ask about *actions* is whether they are in accordance with the appropriate rules; the right question to ask about the *rules* is whether they serve the best interests of everyone concerned.

The rule utilitarian sometimes calculates consequences of particular acts, but only where two rules conflict or where we cannot find an applicable rule. But in most cases the rule utilitarian decides what is right or wrong in particular cases by looking at rules, not directly at consequences. And it is quite reasonable to think that having such rules as "Don't kill innocent people," "Repay those who have helped you," and "Take care of your family" brings more good than not having these rules. Thus it would seem that if Peter had been a rule utilitarian he would have done none of the things that his friends and his subjects objected to.

But perhaps things are not so simple. Can a distinction between act and rule utilitarianism really be maintained? Surely the whole point of having a rule is to serve the greatest good of the greatest number. If a given action breaks a rule but serves the greatest good, when keeping the rule would *not* serve the greatest good, surely it is silly not to perform that action, even if it breaks a rule. If rules are only means to an end—the greatest good—then if they fail to achieve that end they should be discarded.

Furthermore, the rule utilitarian theory as we stated it allows for direct appeals to the "greatest good" principle if rules conflict. But it seems that rules conflict in a great many cases, so many that we shall always be having to appeal to the "greatest good" principle. But if this is so, why bring in the rules at all. Why not just always use the "greatest good" principle?

This objection might be answered by a further modification of rule utilitarianism—what we might call *ranked rule utilitarianism.* This theory would not only state certain general rules (justified by the "greatest good" principle), but would also *rank* these rules in order of importance, again using the "greatest good" principle. Thus, for example, a rule about saving life might take precedence over a rule about saving property. If rules are ranked in this way, so that in case of conflict, we obey rule 1 rather than rule 2, rule 2 rather than rule 3, and so forth, then we do not need to appeal directly to the "greatest good" principle in case of conflict of rules. This would seem to take care of the objection that rules are useless since we would always be appealing to the "greatest good" principle to settle conflicts.

But the first objection remains. If the rules, and the ranking of the rules, are merely means to an end—the greatest good—then what if some action that ought to be done according to the highest ranking rule nevertheless doesn't serve the greatest good. Could this happen? If not, why not? Also, often when we try to state rules there seeems to be a sort of circularity involved in justifying them. Suppose we have a rule such as "Tell the truth." Now, how does telling the truth serve the greatest good? Because it makes people happy? Often it does, but not always. Because it makes people morally better? But that assumes just what we are trying to prove—that telling the truth is a good moral rule. Because truth is valuable in itself? Perhaps; but we seem to be going in a circle. What justifies the rule "Tell the truth"? The fact that telling the truth brings about the greatest good. What good does it bring about? Truthfulness. But now what is the *difference* between saying that "Tell the truth" is a good rule and saying that truthfulness is valuable or good. Again, if someone challenges the assertion that truthfulness is a good thing, how do we convince him? Some goods may be means to other goods, but how do we justify the goodness of *those* goods? Perhaps some sort of appeal to intuition is allowable here, but if so, why not appeal to intuition to justify the rule directly instead of going by way of the "greatest good" principle?

This is not to say that ranked rule utilitarianism—especially in an ideal utilitarian version—does not have some valuable insights. In fact, I will eventually argue for a view that resembles it in many ways. But the closer we get to a satisfactory theory, the less this theory sounds like traditional utilitarianism, and the less important does the "greatest happiness" principle become. So, though utilitarianism may be a step on the way to a satisfactory theory, it is not itself a satisfactory theory.

Another major difficulty with all forms of utilitarianism is the problem of the just distribution of good or happiness. Since the utilitarian principle takes into account only the *amount* of good and the *number* of people benefited, it seems to ignore the moral problems created by unequal distributions. To understand this point clearly, consider an idealized example where good or happiness might be expressed as positive numerical units and evil or unhappiness expressed as negative numerical units, so that we could figure the "net good" or "net happiness" in a situation by adding up positive units and subtracting the negative units. Some of the early utilitarians (Jeremy Bentham for one) thought that such numerical calculations could actually be done with "units" of happiness and unhappiness. Most contemporary utilitarians do not feel that this is a realistic way of dealing with amounts of happiness or unhappiness, but talking in terms of units can be useful for purposes of illustration.

Imagine, then, a country inhabited by two races; call them the Blues and the Greens. The Blues, who are in the majority, have enslaved the Greens, who are bought and sold, are forced to do all the menial work, etc. Not unnaturally, the Blues are quite happy with this arrangement, and although the Greens dislike being slaves, they are not overworked or ill-treated and have a variety of enjoyments available to them. Suppose for the sake of argument that the happiness of the Blues amounts to 10,000 positive units while the unhappiness of the Greens amounts to only 5,000 negative units, so that the "net happiness" is plus 5,000 units. Suppose further that if the Greens were freed from slavery their increased happiness would amount to 5,000 positive units, whereas the unhappiness of the Blues at losing their privileged position would be 1,000 negative units, so that the net happiness of the society would be 4,000 positive units.

Most people would probably be inclined to say that the slaves should be freed because it is not fair for the Blues to exploit the Greens, and even if the Blues would be unhappy at losing their slaves, they have no right to be happy at the expense of the Greens' unhappiness. Furthermore, the total unhappiness under the slavery system is much greater than would be the total unhappiness if the slaves were freed.

But someone committed to the utilitarian principle of "the greatest good of the greatest number" would apparently have to choose the slavery situation because in that situation there is the greatest total good for the greatest number of people. So a utilitarian, even if he were one of the Greens, seemingly ought to oppose freeing the Greens from slavery.

Of course this situation is highly unrealistic; in real life both Blues and Greens would probably be happier in the long run if slavery were abolished. But unfortunately there are many real-life situations where a majority can secure a greater amount of happiness by depriving a minority of rights. In such a situation the utilitarian principle apparently authorizes the majority to exploit the minority, if this leads to the greatest good of the greatest number of people.

Many utilitarians have tried to avoid this conclusion and in fact John Stuart Mill, one of the greatest utilitarian philosophers, gave an impassioned defense of the rights of minorities against the tyranny of the majority. But Mill, as a utilitarian, had to argue for minority rights on the basis that in the long run the protection of these rights would be for the greatest good of the greatest number. There are two drawbacks to this stand, one theoretical and one practical. The theoretical difficulty is that Mill's defense of minority rights is only conditional; *if* there were a case where exploiting the minority for the benefit of the majority *was* for the greatest good of the greatest number, then Mill would have to admit that it was right to exploit the minority.

The practical difficulty is that there do in fact seem to be situations in which the greatest good of the greatest number is served by harming a minority to benefit the majority. In fact a great deal of the exploitation of minorities which does go on goes on because the majority benefit from this exploitation in one way or another. Reformers cannot always show that righting injustices to minorities will pay off for society as a whole. Sometimes the only appeal possible is an appeal to justice or fairness. But it is precisely the appeal to justice or fairness that utilitarianism cannot seem to account for within a utilitarian framework.

Utilitarians have tried in various ways to overcome this difficulty. Here, for example, is one reaction by a prominent contemporary defender of utilitarianism to the kind of crticism sketched above:

> [It has been] suggested that we must maximize the general happiness only if we do so in a *fair* way. An *unfair* way of maximizing the general happiness would be to do so by a method which involved making some people less happy than they might be otherwise. As against this suggestion I would make the following rhetorical objection: if it is rational for me to choose the pain of a visit to the dentist in order to prevent the pain of toothache, why is it not rational of me to choose a pain for Jones, similar to that of my visit to the dentist, if that is the only way in which I can prevent a pain, equal to that of my toothache, for Robinson? Such situations continually occur in war, in mining, and in the fight against disease, when we may often find ourselves in the position of having in the general interest to inflict suffering on good and happy men. However I concede that my objections against fairness as an *ultimate* principle must be rhetori-

> cal only, . . . There are in any case plenty of good utilitarian reasons for adopting the principle of fairness as an important, but not inviolable, rule of thumb.[1]

Smart's suggestion, that a principle of fairness might be derived from the utilitarian principle, is one possible line of defense for the utilitarian. Others have seen the need to have an independent principle of fairness as a supplement to the utilitarian principle. But this creates the problem of what to do in cases of conflict between the principle of fairness and the utilitarian principle. If the utilitarian principle takes precedence, we would have situations like the ones discussed above, where utilitarianism would lead to unfair treatment of minorities. If the principle of justice takes precedence, we would no longer have a utilitarian theory, but rather a mixed theory with a utilitarian element. There may be ways to overcome these difficulties, but it has long been recognized that justice and fairness are especially difficult for the utilitarian to take account of, and that this is one of the greatest objections to utilitarianism.

A related difficulty in utilitarianism is the problem of justifying the "greatest good" principle itself. Several sorts of justification have been offered; we will briefly discuss a few of these. First, one perennially popular view is that by serving the greatest good of the greatest number we always serve our own interests. If true, this would reduce morality to a sort of intelligent self-interest. But fortunately, or unfortunately, it does not seem to be true. Sometimes the good of others can be achieved only by suffering or sacrifice on our part. As we saw in our discussion of egoism, any attempt to deny this either flies in the face of facts known by everyone to be true, or else redefines the notion of something's being in our own interest. If we expand this notion so that doing what is morally good is by definition serving our own interests, then if serving the greatest good is morally good, then serving the greatest good is by definition in our own interest. But in that case it is not an independent argument for the utilitarian principle that it is in our own interest.

Closely related to the attempt to justify the "greatest good" principle as self-serving is one type of religious justification of this principle: that it is only prudent to serve the greatest good of the greatest number because God will reward this sort of behavior. But there is a serious inconsistency in this view. Presumably only a religious believer would use such a justification for the utilitarian principle. But does the religious believer wish to hold that God simply arbitrarily rewards those who, for whatever motive,

[1] J. C. C. Smart, *An Outline of a System of Utilitarian Ethics* (Victoria, Australia: University of Melbourne Press, 1961).

serve the interests of others? Presumably not; presumably the believer wants to hold that God rewards loving, unselfish behavior and punishes selfish behavior. But if the *reason* for serving the good of others is the hope of reward, then there is no real distinction between selfish and unselfish behavior.

A religious believer who has thought the matter through, then, would probably want to hold that loving, altruistic behavior is good in itself and that God uses rewards and punishments to develop such an attitude in us. This is not as paradoxical as it seems; in fact, it is just what parents do in trying to develop unselfishness and responsibility in their children. Great religious teachers have pointed out that the utlimate reward promised to man is loving and being with God forever. Unless we already have an attitude that is loving and unselfish, we will not see this as desirable; the selfish, self-centered person will envy God's power and hate God's superiority. As C.S. Lewis said, "It is safe to promise the pure of heart that they will see God, for only the pure of heart would want to."

Once we realize this, we can see that attempts to justify the "greatest good" principle as simple prudence, on the ground of God's rewards, is inconsistent with the kind of religious views which would be held by intelligent believers. This does not mean that there cannot be religious grounds for morality. A believer may hold that we should be loving and unselfish because we ourselves have received so much from God, or because "God is love" and we should try to be like Him. Thus the religious believer may have arguments for morality which are bound up with his whole religious outlook. But probably, like most religious believers, he wants to say that nonbelievers can be guilty of sin and that religion brings to them a way to deal with sin, a message about the forgiveness of sin. If so, the believer must hold that there is some way independent of religion by which men can know what is right and wrong. (St. Paul, for example, held that non-Jews, who were unaware of the revelation of the Ten Commandments, etc., to the Jews, nevertheless were guilty of sin because they "had the law of God written in their hearts.") Thus any attempt to base moral principles only on religious revelation seems to be in fact inconsistent with the usual kinds of religious belief!

How, then, might we justify the utilitarian principle if not on prudential or religious grounds? The most hopeful possibility seems to be an appeal to some sort of moral insight or intuition common to all men (for the religious believer this would be Paul's "law" written on men's hearts). But if we make an appeal to moral insight or intuition, we seem to find a number of moral principles, not just the utilitarian principle. In the next chapter we will look at some accounts of these principles and probe more deeply into the notion of moral insight or intuition.

DISCUSSION QUESTIONS

1. How might a hedonistic utilitarian reply to the criticisms made of his theory in this chapter?
2. What goods besides happiness should an ideal utilitarian take into account?
3. Does rule utilitarianism give a reasonable account of how we arrive at laws and social customs?
4. Give a case where two rules justified on utilitarian grounds might conflict.
5. What moral rules are hard to justify on purely utilitarian grounds? Why?
6. What rules might an ideal rule utilitarian arrive at? How might he rank those rules?
7. Give a case where the greatest good of the greatest number conflicts with an individual's interests. What difficulty would this create for the utilitarian?
8. Could a Christian have a purely utilitarian moral philosophy? Why or why not?
9. What advantages does utilitarianism have over ethical egoism?
10. How might an intelligent utilitarian criticize Prince Peter's conduct from a utilitarian point of view?

FURTHER READINGS

EWING, A. C., *Ethics,* pp. 36-48. New York: The Free Press, 1953.

FRANKENA, WILLIAM, *Ethics* (2nd. ed.), pp. 34-61. Englewood Cliffs, N.J.: Prentice-Hall, Inc., 1973.

FRANKENA, WILLIAM, and JOHN GRANROSE, *Introductory Readings in Ethics.* Englewood Cliffs, N.J.: Prentice-Hall, Inc., 1974:

BENTHAM, JEREMY, "Hedonistic Act Utilitarianism," pp. 130-137.

BRANDT, RICHARD, "Toward a Creditable Form of Utilitarianism," pp. 154-164.

DONAGAN, ALAN, "Is There a Creditable Form of Utilitarianism?" pp. 164-171.

SIDGWICK, HENRY, "Utilitarianism and Justice," pp. 172-175.

SINGER, MARCUS, "Generalization in Ethics," pp. 143-145.

WARNOCK, G. J., "Moral Virtues and Principles," pp. 192-200.

SELLARS, WILFRED, and JOHN HOSPERS, *Readings in Ethical Theory* (2nd ed.). New York: Appleton-Century-Crofts, 1970:

LYONS, DAVID, "Utilitarian Generalization," pp. 451-469.
MOORE, G. E., "Utilitarianism," pp. 431-451.
SOBEL, J. HOWARD, "Generalization Arguments," pp. 548-564.

4 Ethical Rules: Love or Legalism?

One day not too long after he had come to State University, Tom Brown sat down and looked squarely at his financial problems. He had a job tending the experimental animals for the psychology department; this took care of his basic financial needs with a little left over for enjoyment. But all of a sudden a number of demands for money had descended on him. He had promised his parents, now dead, that he would look after his brother Harry, and Harry badly needed ten dollars to pay a transfer fee so he could change his dormitory room. Tom knew that Harry's insomnia was genuine and that unless he could get away from that room near the elevator he would never get enough sleep, but they couldn't convince the dormitory authorities, and Harry would have to pay the transfer fee. Old Ted, the former family handyman, was in need of money again—probably his own fault as usual, but Ted had no one else to turn to. Ten would probably tide him over for a while, too. But then there was kindly old Dr. Ed, who had done so much good for the poor people in the town, never asking for any return. Now he needed to go to Arizona for his asthma and Tom had been asked to pledge ten dollars toward the fund being collected for the purpose. There were few enough who remembered the old man and Tom knew his contribution was really needed. But then there was Tom's oldest friend, Dick, who had done so much for him in the past: he was asking for a ten-dollar loan and Dick wouldn't ask unless he really needed it. Worst of all, Tom, in a weak moment, had taken ten dollars from the desk of his absentminded roommate, Paul. In one sense, Paul would never miss the money: he would never know where it had gone and would never suspect Tom. But in the sense of *needing* it, Paul was just as badly off as any of the others. And hardly in the same class, but still tempting, was that ten-dollar art book that Tom would enjoy owning so much and which would really help him in his Art Appreciation class. Of course there was that fellow Peter down the hall who seemed to have more money than most students, and who was always leaving his wallet in the changing room after handball. . . .

Tom gritted his teeth and took out a sheet of paper. He would *not* steal from Peter, even to pay back Paul. If he did that, he might just as well steal from someone else to pay Peter, and so on indefinitely. What he would do was ask for overtime work. He knew he could handle it though it would cut into his recreation time. With the extra money, the first thing he would do would be to pay back the money he had stolen from Paul. Even Harry would have to wait until he had done that. But Harry would come next; he would explain to Dick, and Dick would understand. After Harry's fee had been payed he would loan Dick the ten. And he could pledge ten dollars toward Dr. Ed's trip if they would wait till Dick had paid him back or till the next paycheck, whichever came first. Poor old Ted would have to wait a while, but Tom promised himself that he'd help Ted before buying that book. Ted wasn't very deserving, he supposed, but he was sick and old and had no one else to turn to. But if nothing else came up he might eventually be able to get that book!

I have used variations of this story on a number of students, and the decisions made by Tom reflect the judgments made by the great majority of the students. Of course the situation is a highly artificial one, with each person's need for the money being the same, and the amount of money being the same in each case. Also, of course, people need many kinds of help from us—our work, our time, even a kind word or smile—and not just monetary help. There are many kinds of repayment we might have to make which are not financial reparation—an apology, telling the truth about a lie we've told. But as more and more cases are considered, a great many people would agree with the English philosopher W.D. Ross that we do have moral duties and that they can be classified in roughly the following way:

> (1) Some duties rest on previous acts of my own. These duties seem to include two kinds, (a) those resting on a promise or what may fairly be called an implicit promise, such as the implicit undertaking not to tell lies which seems to be implied in the act of entering into conversation (at any rate by civilized men), or of writing books that purport to be history and not fiction. These may be called the duties of fidelity. (b) Those resting on a previous wrongful act. These may be called the duties of reparation. (2) Some rest on previous acts of other men, i.e., services done by them to me. These may be loosely described as the duties of gratitude. (3) Some rest on the fact or possibility of a distribution of pleasure or happiness (or of the means thereto) which is not in accordance with the merit of the persons concerned; in such cases there arises a duty to upset or prevent such a distribution. These are the duties of justice. (4) Some rest on the mere fact that there are other beings in the world whose condition we can make better in respect of virtue, or of intelligence, or of pleasure. These are the duties of beneficence. (5) Some rest on the fact that we can improve our own condition in respect of virtue or of intelligence. These are the duties of self-improvement. (6) I think that we should distinguish from (4) the duties that may be summed up under the title of "not injuring others." No doubt to injure others is incidentally to fail to do them good; but it seems to me clear than non-maleficence is apprehended as a duty distinct from that of beneficence, and as a duty of a more stringent character. It will be noted that this alone among the types of duty has been stated in a negative way. An attempt might no doubt be made to state this duty, like the others, in a positive way. It might be said that it is really the duty to prevent ourselves from acting either from an inclination to harm others or from an inclination to seek our own pleasure, in doing which we should incidentally harm them. But on reflection it seems clear that the primary duty here is the duty not to harm others, this being a duty whether or not we have an inclination that if followed would lead to our harming them; and that when we have such an inclination the primary duty not to harm others gives rise to a consequential duty to resist the inclination. The recognition of this duty of non-maleficence is the first step on the way to the recognition of the duty of beneficence; and that accounts for the prominence of the commands "thou shalt not kill," "thou shalt not commit adultery," "thou shalt not steal," "thou shalt not bear false witness," in so early a code as the Decalogue. But even when we have come to recognize the duty of beneficence, it appears to me that the duty of non-maleficence is recognized as a distinct one, and as *prima facie* more binding. We should not in general consider it justifiable to kill one person in order to keep another alive, or to steal from one in order to give alms to another.[1]

In our imaginary case, we could say that Tom's decision not to rob

[1] W. D. Ross, *The Right and the Good* (Oxford: Oxford University Press, 1930), p. 22. Quoted by permission of the Oxford University Press, Oxford.

Peter reflects Ross's (6), the duty of non-maleficence; his decision to repay Paul reflects (1(b)), the duty of reparation; his decision to help Harry, (1(a)), the duty of fidelity. Tom's decision to loan Dick the money he needed reflects (2), the duty of gratitude; his decision to help Ed reflects (3), the duty of justice; and his decision to help Ted reflects (4), the duty of beneficence. Insofar as he wanted the art book to improve his knowledge of art, it would seem that his decision to buy it would reflect (5), the duty of self-improvement.

Now any of these duties can come into conflict in a given situation; in our imaginary situation they *all* come into conflict. For this reason Ross calls them *prima facie* duties (*prima facie* is a Latin phrase meaning "at first glance" or "on first examination"—as we speak of a *prima facie* case against a defendant. Ross uses the phrase in this way in the passage above although he does not in that passage use the term *prima facie* duties). In Ross's view our genuine moral duty in any situation has to be arrived at by weighing our *prima facie* duties and deciding which is most important. For example, suppose I am driving with my wife on icy streets to a meeting I had promised to attend. The car skids into another, damaging the other car slightly but injuring my wife seriously. My *prima facie* duties in this situation are to get my wife to the hospital, to give my name and insurance company to the other driver, and to get to my appointment. Obviously my duty to get my wife to the hospital is by far the most important, followed probably by giving my name and insurance company to the other driver. But if the appointment is a matter of life or death, it might be more important than giving my name to the other driver, and in extreme cases could even be more important than getting my wife to the hospital. (Suppose, for example, we were rushing to the Governor with evidence that would prevent my wife's father from being unjustly executed.)

Thus Ross has two important points to make. First, there is a range of duties generally recognized; keeping promises, making reparation for injuries, etc. Second, these duties can conflict and our real duty in the situation depends on which is the most important or, as Ross usually says, "most stringent" (that is, most binding or serious). Both points are extremely important and quite easy to misunderstand. If you talk of moral duties or moral rules, people will often point out that there is wide disagreement as to what people ought to do in a given case and that no moral rule is such that it ought *never* to be broken. But Ross's theory can take care of both points. His rules give *prima facie* duties, not "absolute" duties; and disagreement in a particular case can be due to disagreement as to which of our *prima facie* duties is more important.

How do we decide in those cases where the rules themselves conflict? Ross himself is inclined to say that we must judge each such case individually, that no rules can be given for choosing between rules in case of conflict. He does, however, say that in general some duties are more stringent than others. He suggests that the duty of non-maleficence usually overrides the others, and that duties of fidelity come next in importance. If Ross merely means that no absolute rules can be given which will enable us to make decisions mechanically without any need for judgment, he would seem to be right. But if we do not insist on hard and fast rules, but merely attempt to give a ranking which holds "other things being equal," then it might be possible to argue that there are some generally acceptable standards by which we can measure the importance or stringency of a *prima facie* duty. It would seem that a ranking of duties or obligations such as the following would be acceptable, subject to certain qualifications:

1. Not to harm others
2. To make reparation for harm done by us
3. To keep our commitments
4. To repay our benefactors
5. To treat people at least as well as they deserve to be treated
6. To do some good to some people, deserving or not
7. To improve ourselves in some ways

As you can see, this is the ranking Tom followed in our story. In the story, everyone's need was about equal, and the amount of good involved was about equal in each case. In a situation where needs or goods were unequal, different decisions might be reasonable. If a grateful patient left Dr. Ed a fortune, Tom could forget his contribution to Dr. Ed and help Ted. If his friend Dick would starve or go to jail for lack of the ten dollars, this would be more important than Harry's dormitory problem. But there are some limits to the extent to which such considerations can outweigh the ranking. Tom is not entitled to rob Peter to buy books, no matter how much good the books would do Tom. If Tom owes money to someone, he is not entitled to refuse to repay his debt because the money would do more good to starving refugees somewhere.

There are other considerations too. Causing a person pain is certainly one way of harming him, but keeping him in ignorance or deceiving him on an important matter may harm him more, and corrupting him morally may harm him even more. In terms of benefits, most of us admire a good teacher, who makes us wiser, more than a good comedian or a good cook who merely increases our enjoyment. And we admire most of all a person who by teaching or example has helped us become morally better. Thus if we divide goods into moral goodness, wisdom or understanding, and happiness or pleasure, moral goodness seems better than wisdom, and wisdom better than pleasure. This ranking will affect our judgment about obligations; for example, a commitment to educate a child may outweigh an obligation not to make the child unhappy, or a duty not to injure someone's moral character may outweigh what might otherwise be an obligation to give him certain knowledge.

As was said earlier, the ranking of obligations we have suggested represents an "other things being equal" rule for deciding which obligation is more important. Other things being equal, a specific promise to help Harry outweighs a general obligation to repay Dick for past benefits. But if other things are not equal—if, for example, Dick needs the money much more desperately than Harry—another decision may be in order. But other things usually are equal and there are not an indefinitely large number of things which can affect a moral decision. It is not difficult to list at least the main kinds of morally relevant considerations.

The great advantage of this kind of moral theory is that it seems to correspond very closely to the way in which we actually make moral decisions and argue about moral issues. As J.R. Lucas points out:

> If I was arguing with a man, and he did not allow that causing pain was *a* reason for action's being wrong, that is, he did not *see* the relevance of the fact that the action caused pain, I think I should break off the argument with him. Almost all our serious moral arguments—on capital punishment, on divorce, on family and professional obligations—are carried on within a context of fairly wide agreement on what considerations are relevant to the issue. The problem is what weight to attach to the various considerations. We cannot carry on one of these arguments with a man who does not see that there is any argument against killing people, or making them unhappy, or neglecting one's family or abandoning one's vocation.[2]

On the other hand, we hardly ever make moral decisions or argue about moral issues by merely figuring consequences without regard to obligations of the kind described by Ross. As Ross himself points out:

> The essential defect of the "ideal utilitarian" theory is that it ignores, or at least does not do full justice to, the highly personal character of duty. If the only duty is to produce the maximum of good, the question who is to have the good—whether it is myself, or my benefactor, or a person to whom I have made a promise to confer that good on him, or a mere fellow man to whom I stand in no such special relation—should make no difference to my having a duty to produce that good. But we are all in fact sure that it makes a vast difference.[3]

[2] J. R. Lucas, "Ethical Intuitionism II," *Philosophy*, XLVI, no. 175 (January 1971), 9-10.

[3] Ross, *The Right and The Good*, p. 22.

Of course the ideal utilitarian could try to include such things as keeping promises, making reparation for injuries, etc., as goods which we ought to bring about. He could then say that some goods outweigh other goods, and should be brought about if we have a choice between them and the lesser goods. But this would seem to be just a theory like Ross's, put in terms of goods instead of in terms of duties or obligations.

Since a theory along the general lines of Ross's seems to be the best account of our moral reasoning, there is not an *objection* to ideal utilitarianism on the grounds that it arrives at a theory like that given by Ross. In fact, if anyone starting from a generally utilitarian point of view modifies that view until it comes close to a Rossian view, they would seem to be making a step in the right direction. But a "utilitarian" view modified in this way would be quite different from what we usually think of as utilitarianism. Nor is it at all clear that we can arrive at a Ross-type view by purely utilitarian considerations. When a utilitarian begins to distinguish one kind of pleasure as better than another he is no longer a pure hedonistic utilitarian. And similarly, if an ideal utilitarian begins to talk about "promise keeping" as a value rather than talking about the practice of keeping promises as leading to some value, he may no longer be a utilitarian at all, for even rule utilitarianism is teleological or consequential: it justifies practices in terms of results; it does not regard practices as valuable in themselves.

In addition, utilitarianism seems to be committed to the idea that the right action is the action which brings about the greatest total good. But unless we mean by "total good" something quite different than most utilitarians mean, a Rossian view will sometimes regard an action as right even if it does not bring about the greatest total good. If I have stolen money from a fairly well-to-do person, it would probably always be true that it would do more good to give the money to CARE than to repay my theft; but a Rossian view puts reparation above unrequired benevolence. To say that the "value" of making reparation must be figured into the "total good" is to use utilitarian language for a quite un-utilitarian point of view.

Let us now turn to the question of how we can justify moral rules. We have spoken previously about "moral intuition" or moral insight. What do we mean by moral intuition? Is it like one of our physical senses? By our sense of sight we can tell whether things are light or dark, and tell the shape and color of objects. Do we have a "moral sense" that tells us that some actions are morally good, some morally bad?

The view that a "moral sense" is not unlike our other senses is an attractive one, but there seem to be serious difficulties with it. If this view is true, then it would seem to follow that moral goodness and badness are like colors—qualities which something could have or lack regardless of whatever other qualities it might have or lack. But this does not seem to be true. Two chairs can be alike in every respect except that one of them is yellow and the other is blue. But two actions cannot be alike in every respect except that one of them is good and the other bad. The goodness or badness of an action seems to be necessarily connected with other qualities linked to it. Moral goodness and badness seem to be what some moral philosophers call *supervenient* qualities: they *follow from* (or "supervene on") the possession of other qualities in some way. "Seeing" that an action is good or bad is a *judgment,* not merely a perception. But if this is so, then moral intuition is not a "moral sense."

If we know what is right or wrong by a judgment which is based on the nonmoral aspects of an action, person, etc., then moral intuition is more like the other judgments made by our reason than it is like sense perception. Any defensible theory of moral intuition, then, will have to take account of this. A satisfactory theory must answer the question, "How (if at all) can we arrive at correct, objective moral *judgments?*"

Let us look back to the classification of ethical theories at the end of Chapter 1. Subjectivism, the theory that right and wrong depend on individual choice or will, will obviously not give us a way of arriving at objective moral judgments. Social relativism, the theory that right and wrong depend on the will of society, still does not give us something that is truly objective since it merely substitutes the choice or whim of the group for that of an individual. The Divine Will theory, too, leaves us without an objective right and wrong, since if this theory were correct it would seem that God could change His commands tomorrow and make what is now right to be wrong and what is now wrong to be right.

The benefit theories—egoism, utilitarianism, and the Divine Glory theory—all give us something objective, though perhaps hard to discover and apply. What will really benefit me in the long run? What will benefit society? What is to the glory of God? There are simple instances where answers to these questions seem easy, but there are many complex cases where it is not easy to see where benefit to ourself or others lie. Furthermore, there are unanswered questions about benefit. Even if it is in some sense obvious that I will want to benefit myself, is it so obvious that I will want to benefit myself at great cost to others? But why should I make my aim the benefit of others—why should I sacrifice myself to them? Or on the Divine Glory theory, why should I try to glorify God (especially if there is nothing I can do that God can't do better).

In trying to answer these questions we seem forced in the direction of some theory based on the nature of man. I think that this is the right direction—that our moral ideas and moral judgments are based on certain facts about human nature. Because we are beings of a certain sort, it is right for us to act in certain ways and wrong for us to act in other ways. This is in one sense a naturalistic theory, since it bases right and wrong on facts about our nature. So if this theory is to be successful it must answer the question posed by Hume and others: How can we get an "ought" (a statement about what I *ought* to do or *ought* not to do) out of an "is" (a statement about the way human nature *is*)?

I will try to answer this question in due course, but before we try to base morality on human nature we must face the objection that there is no general human nature, that individual differences are so great that if we base right and wrong on human nature, then right and wrong will be different for each person. (This is the view which we called "ethical individualism" in Chapter 1.)

We will look more closely at one version of ethical individualism in the next chapter, but let us take a preliminary look at it in terms of this question of human nature. Is it really true that each of us is so different that there is no common human nature? Start on a simple physical level. All human beings are born in the same way; all need air and water and food. If they get too warm or too cold, they die or at least suffer damage. All human beings need a certain amount of rest, but also need a certain amount of activity. In other words, the basic physical needs of human beings are the same for all.

But similarities do not stop here. All human beings have social needs. They need to communicate with other human beings; they need to have some acceptance from others; and they need cooperation from others to live a fully human life. It is true that an occasional human being becomes a hermit, but he usually depends on civilization for supplies and various kinds of support. A hermit reading a book by the light of a kerosene lamp may not have contact with other human beings in the usual way, but he is being helped and supported by others nevertheless. A hermit who tried to be totally independent of society would shortly sink to a purely animal level. The occasional religious hermit feels himself to be in close contact with God through his prayers, and usually feels concern for other human beings and prays for them. Thus, Aristotle was right in thinking that a man without society would live either on a subhuman or a superhuman level—"either a beast or a god."

Related to social needs but different from them are personal needs: for love, for friendship, for affection. Almost all human beings feel the need of some close relationships, such as erotic love and family affection. Other needs are for friendships based on mutual respect and common interests, and for affectionate or familiar relationships with a somewhat wider circle. Of course some human beings are deprived of these personal needs or deprive themselves of them. But for a human life to be fully satisfactory and fully human, it would seem that it must contain satisfaction of personal and social needs as well as of purely physical needs. This much is common to all human beings.

Within this basic similarity there is, of course, immense variety. We like different foods, enjoy different kinds of communication, love different people. Within the survivable range of temperatures, some like it hot and some like it cold. Within a general framework of acceptance by others, some long for fame while some prefer obscurity. The kind of friends and the kind of friendship we like vary immensely. In the area of activity some like more and some like less, and the kinds of activities preferred are extremely diverse. In cooperating with others, some like to lead, some are content to follow, and others prefer independence. Some people are gregarious and affectionate, others prefer cooler relationships with their acquaintances.

But none of these differences disturbs the basic similarities on which morality is based. Consider someone who breaks one or more of the Ross Rules which we have discussed in this chapter. If people harm others and make no attempt to repair the harm, if they break commitments, fail to repay benefactors, deal with others unfairly, do not help others when they can, and fail to improve themselves in any way, then how can they expect others to communicate with them, to accept them, to cooperate with them? Or how can they expect love, friendship, or affection?

There are possible ways of evading these consequences. You may have social and personal relationships with a small group while injuring or cheating the larger society. You may be a successful hypocrite and attain respect or friendship on the basis of qualities people *think* you have. Or you can secure apparent respect, cooperation, even apparent friendship or affection by making yourself feared and bullying others into doing what you want them to, or by becoming rich and buying cooperation or affection. Whether such "solutions" are satisfactory in the long run is another matter.

We will explore these points in more detail later, but first let us turn briefly to the question of whether we are going illegitimately from an "is"—human beings have these needs—to an "ought"—human beings ought to obey the Ross Rules. Begin by considering a very common case where we get "ought" from "is" without any problems. These are the cases of "instrumental" or "hypothetical" oughts, as for example: "If you want to get to Europe cheaply you ought to take a charter flight," or "If you want to avoid colds you ought to take Vitamin C." No one is puzzled by "getting 'ought' out of 'is' " in cases like these; the "ought" indicates a *means* to a desired *end*.

However, "instrumental" or "hypothetical" oughts are dependent on the conditions stated. If you have no desire to go to Europe, or if money is no object, then it is not true that you ought to take a charter flight. If you prefer having a cold to dosing yourself with vitamins, then it is not true that you ought to take Vitamin C. The "you ought to" depends on the "if you want to . . ." and if you *don't* want to then it isn't true that you ought to. Thus many moralists, notably Kant, have thought that moral "oughts" are quite different from hypothetical or instrumental "oughts," since moral "oughts" seem to be unconditional, not depending on what we want or choose.

But to say that moral oughts are not conditional on your wants does not mean that they are not conditional at all. Needs as well as wants can create "hypothetical" or "conditional" oughts. However, since the need is taken for granted, it is often not an "if" but a "since" that is expressed: "Since (if) you need sleep you *ought* to get some," or "You ought to eat because (if) you need food."

Some needs are more constant than others. After you have slept well you do not for a while need sleep. After you have eaten well you do not for a while need to eat. But after you have taken a breath you need to exhale and take another. Similarly, social and personal needs vary with time. After getting all the instruction and advice I can I may wish to carry out a project alone. After an evening with friends I may enjoy walking home alone. But to go permanently without friends or the co-operation of others would damage something in us as surely as going permanently without food would kill us.

So far I have put this point in a negative way: If you *break* the Ross Rules, then you will *not* be able to satisfy social and personal needs. Can this point be put in a positive way? Do I want to say that our motive for keeping moral rules should be that keeping moral rules enables us to satisfy our social and personal needs. My answer is a qualified "yes." Our need to be accepted and liked by others is to some extent the foundation of ethical rules.

This might seem to reduce morality to an egoistic calculation, but it does not. To want respect and friendship from others, and to be willing to act in such a way that we will get it, is already to have moved away from pure egoism, for the pure egoist considers no one's feelings but his own. To value others' respect or friendship is not to be a pure egoist.

Again, once we realize the full meaning of, say, respect or friendship, we realize that real respect or real friendship cannot be bought or be secured by bullying. Only a real consideration for others will bring about real respect or friendship. And it is the real thing, not substitutes, that we need.

We will return to this matter of the foundations of morality at the end of the book, but for the moment let it suffice for us to see that although Ross is correct in saying that we have "moral intuitions," tha is not the end of the story. Moral intuitions must be based on something, and I have argued that they are based on human nature and human needs. It may be that our view of human nature will be very much affected by our view of the world as a whole; this is a topic we will consider in due course. But for the moment we will take a closer look at one variety of ethical individualism—an attempt to have ethics without rules.

DISCUSSION QUESTIONS

1. Has Ross neglected any important moral duties? Which ones? Could these be special cases of one of his rules?
2. Does Ross's view that conflicts of rules must be decided by intuition weaken the value of his rules? Why or why not?
3. What problem does the idea of a *prima facie* rule try to solve? Does it succeed?
4. What kind of factors might change the proposed ranking of the Ross Rules? Mention a specific case.
5. Could a case be made that we have a "moral sense" which tells us what is right and wrong, just as our sense of sight tells us what is light or dark? Why or why not?
6. Are there other supervenient qualities besides evaluational qualities like "right," "beautiful," etc.? If you think there are, name some. If you think there are not, why do you think so?
7. If moral rules were based on human nature, could we change them by changing human nature? Would it follow that everyone would know them without being taught them? Why or why not?
8. Do any moral rules seem self-evident to you? What are they?
9. What difficulty does the view that the universe is absurd and meaningless create for the idea of absolute moral rules?
10. What changes in Tom Brown's situation might occur which would change Tom's decisions about how to use his money (e.g., if Harry's insomnia was making him ill, should Tom still repay Paul first?)?

FURTHER READINGS

Ewing, A. C., *Ethics*, pp. 49-60. New York: The Free Press, 1953.

Frankena, William, *Ethics* (2nd ed.), pp. 23-33. Englewood Cliffs, N.J.: Prentice-Hall, Inc., 1973.

FRANKENA, WILLIAM, and JOHN GRANROSE, *Introductory Readings in Ethics.* Englewood Cliffs, N.J.: Prentice-Hall, Inc., 1974:

BLANSHARD, BRAND, "Rightness and Goodness," pp. 90–94.

ROSS, W. D., "What Makes Right Acts Right?" pp. 81-90.

SELLARS, WILFRED, and JOHN HOSPERS, *Readings in Ethical Theory* (2nd ed.). New York: Appleton-Century-Crofts, 1970:

BLANSHARD, BRAND, " 'Good,' 'Right,' 'Ought,' 'Bad,' " pp. 222-240.

ROSS, W. D., "The Meaning of Good," pp. 152-169.

———, "The Meaning of Right," pp. 106-115.

5 Situation Ethics: Ethics Without Rules

"Did you want to see me, Bob?"

Reverend Robert Butler looked up from his desk as his assistant pastor, Reverend Carl Crozier, came into the room, as usual without knocking. "Yes, Carl, I think that we'd better have a talk." Butler fingered the pipe on his desk, wishing as he often did at awkward moments, that he hadn't given up smoking and could fill and light his pipe to give himself time to think. "Carl, its about some of the things you've been saying in sermons and counseling our parishioners. You seem to have gone pretty well overboard on this "situation ethics" business. No moral rules, just act in a spirit of 'loving concern,' that's how I understand your position."

"That's right, Bob," said Crozier with a smile that was friendly but also a bit superior. "I know that when you were in the seminary Ethics was all rules and legalism, but I think that we now have a deeper understanding of real morality. It isn't just due to Fletcher, either, although his book *Situation Ethics* was one excellent expression of the new ideas. We've come to realize that rigid following of rules and legalistic hair-splitting in the face of human needs and miseries is actually immoral, not moral."

"But look here, Carl" said Butler. "You're doing precisely what I object to in many people who hold your position. You talk as if the only alternative to *your* position were a position of rigid legalism. I don't know what your sources of information are about what was taught at the seminary in 'my day,' but remember I was there and you weren't. I was certainly taught, and have tried to teach others, a concern for human needs and human miseries. But one human need is the need to know what to expect from others, and one source of human misery is the disregarding of moral rules by others. For instance, I prefer a man who won't lie because he holds that it's against God's law to bear false witness, to a man who'd say anything he felt was best in the circumstances. I've seen the harm that even well-intentioned lies can do. Moreover, the man who tells me the truth lets me have the facts I need to make up my own mind, while the man who tells me a comforting lie takes it upon himself to make up my mind for me."

Crozier flushed. "I suppose you're thinking of old Mrs. Garigan. I know you disagreed with me about that, but I still think it was in accordance with a spirit of loving concern not to tell her she was dying."

Butler lifted his hand. "It wasn't just not telling her, Carl; you told her, and encouraged her relatives to tell her, that she was going to recover. I don't doubt that saying that made it more comfortable for the relatives, and even in one sense for her. Certainly when I told her the truth she broke down for a while, and everyone was uncomfortable and unhappy. But I was with her at the end, and she thanked me for telling her."

"All right," interrupted Crozier, "in that case you may have been right. But surely there are cases where it's right to lie. Would you agree with Kant that you should tell the truth to a madman who asks you the whereabouts of his enemy in order to kill him?"

Butler leaned forward. "Not necessarily," he said. "I agree that there can be cases where we have a conflict of obligations, and the more important obligation can overrule the less important one. Sometimes we're faced with a choice of evils and all that we can do is try to choose the lesser evil. But I do insist that there has to be a clear conflict of actual obligations or a forced choice between actual evils."

"But if you allow that ethical rules aren't unbreakable, you've really become a situationist," said Crozier.

"Not so fast," replied Butler. "I agree that moral rules can come into conflict and that a greater obligation can overrule a lesser one. But there's more than that to situation ethics. You want to say that each situation is different and that no rules can be given. You want to say that any action can be right if it's done in a certain spirit—what you call a spirit of loving concern. My objection to that is that it's awfully easy to fool yourself about the spirit in which you do things. Young Jimmy Fredericks is rather a disciple of yours, isn't he Carl? And yet I can't say that his behavior towards his girlfriends or towards his family has gotten any better. Worse, if anything. But now his conscience no longer bothers him, because he's convinced himself that he's acting in a spirit of loving concern. It's not so easy to tell yourself that you're truthful or honest or fair or kind when your actions show plainly the reverse. But our motives are easier to fool ourselves about."

Crozier frowned. "I don't think you're being fair to Jimmy, but let me put it in terms that will be more familiar to you. Don't you agree that the greatest commandments are to love God and our neighbor? What's that but a commandment to loving concern?"

Butler nodded. "That's certainly a good point, Carl, but I think that we have to ask ourselves what love of neighbor comes to in practical terms. To love our neighbor is not to harm him, to treat him justly and kindly. More specifically, not to kill, not to steal, not to bear false witness, not to commit adultery, not to covet. Loving your neighbor isn't something different from keeping moral rules or commandments. Keeping the commandments is the *why* we love God and our neighbor. Now consider Christ and the rich young man. . . ."

This argument can be carried on in terms of specific religious teachings, as the Reverend Butler was beginning to do in our story. But we can also approach situation ethics from a purely philosophical point of view, as an attempt to do justice to certain elements in our moral experience. Seen in this way, situation ethics has a positive and a negative side. The negative side is a criticism of any ethical system based on rules, and we must ask ourselves whether the Reverend Butler in our story was right in suggesting that situation ethics gains a cheap victory by attacking an exaggerated form of rule theory which reasonable rule theorists would not defend. The positive side of situation ethics is its view of morality as acting in a certain spirit, and we will have to ask ourselves whether a reply can be made to Butler's criticisms on this point.

The negative side of the situationist view looks fairly convincing at first glance. If we think of such moral rules as "Do not lie," "Do not steal," "Do not commit adultery," it would seem that there are some circumstances which might justify breaking such rules. Thus, if the situationist confines himself to saying that no rules of this kind are absolutely unbreakable, it would seem that most people's moral intuitions would be in agreement. For instance, suppose you are present when a woman you know, Mrs. Cratchit, has a heart attack. Your knowledge of her condition tells you that unless she gets to the hospital immediately she will die. At the curb, with the keys in, is the car of your disagreeable neighbor, Mr. Scrooge. You know that Scrooge is so selfish that he would never consent to have his car used, but it is the only vehicle which can get Mrs. Cratchit to the hospital in time. In this case, surely it is *right* to take the car, even if it violates the moral rule against stealing and annoys Scrooge very much.

But a person who takes the "hierarchical" view of ethical rules, discussed in the last chapter, can readily grant cases like this. What he will insist is that there must be a clear conflict of obligations or a forced choice of evils before we violate a moral rule. It is not that no moral rules can be given which apply to complex situations, but rather that in complex situations more than one moral rule may apply, and there may be a conflict of obligations. The holder of absolutistic theories of moral rules—theories that say moral rules must never be broken—seem to ignore the fact that conflicts of obligation can and do arise. Against the absolutistic view, the hierarchist and the situationist can make common cause.

But the situationist, in reaction against an absolutistic view, has actually rushed to the other extreme. The fact that there can be conflicting obligations refutes his extreme view as well as the absolutistic view. For if each situation were unique, and there were no general rules, then there could not really be conflicting obligations. The reason that cases like that of Mrs. Cratchit are cases of *conflict* is that there are *prima facie* obligations which are incompatible. Consider a parallel situation. Suppose that you have a college admissions officer who has no rules to go by and is simply told to use his own judgment about whom to admit to the college. He can have a hard time making up his mind—he can be pulled in various directions by various features of the situation. But he cannot have a conflict of *obligations*. On the other hand, an admissions officer who has rules to go by may be obliged to admit a student by one rule and be forbidden to admit him by another rule. Perhaps one rule says that all high school graduates must be admitted and another rule says that no one can be admitted who cannot pass a qualifying test. This officer will have an actual conflict of obligations, and unless he has some way of resolving the conflict he will be in trouble. He will break a rule if he admits a certain student, but also break a rule if he refuses to admit him.

Only if one rule outranks another rule, or if he has some other way of coming to a decision, can he resolve the conflict. And it seems that our actual moral experience is that we do have moral conflicts, and they are often agonizingly difficult to resolve. So our situation is more like that of the second admissions officer than it is like that of the first one.

Some supporters of situation ethics would argue that there cannot be real conflicts of moral rules because basically there is only one moral rule. "Love your neighbor" and "Do to others as you would want them to do to you" have been offered as candidates for this one basic moral rule. And certainly such principles seem to express something very basic to morality. But an action that helps one person may harm another (Mrs. Cratchit gets to the hospital, but Mr. Scrooge misses a business appointment). To whom should we apply the rule "Do as you would be done by"? Furthermore, as the Reverend Butler pointed out in our story, not harming others, treating them fairly, treating them kindly, and so on, seem to be what love of neighbor comes to in practical theory.

Supporters of a rule view of ethics would want to point out that we can express moral rules at various levels of generality. We can give very general rules like "Love your neighbor," more specific rules like "Do not harm other persons," or yet more specific rules like "Do not murder" or "Do not steal," which mention specific kinds of harm people do to one another. The more general the rule the freer it is from obvious exceptions, but the more specific the rule the more help it is in dealing with specific problems. For admitting students to a college, "Admit all well-qualified students" would be relatively free from exceptions, but not much help in deciding cases. "Admit only students with a score of over 85 on the present college admission tests" would be extremely specific, but there might be many good reasons for making exceptions.

Interestingly enough, what is often done in, for example, college admissions, is to have a framework of rules with provisions for exceptions and modifications to be made by intelligent and impartial persons (such as a faculty committee or some similar group). It seems likely that there is some point in the moral reasoning where the individual judgment or conscience must make the final decision, within the framework of moral rules but not simply as the result of a mechanical application of moral rules. What situation ethics seems to do is to seize on this element of judgment as if it were the whole story, instead of just one important part of it.

Of course some situations are so clear-cut that there is no particular scope for ethical judgment. Sometimes it may or may not be justifiable to take human life—for instance, to defend other human lives. But if a man steps on your toe while you are both looking at the Grand Canyon, it is plainly not justifiable to push him over a cliff merely because he has annoyed you. It is easy enough to cite instances where ethical judgments are completely unambiguous by simply building a lack of conflicting considerations into the description of the case. It is always immoral to torture people to death for no other reason than that you dislike their appearance. It is always wrong to break important promises just because and only because you are feeling lazy . . . and so on. Of course, real life cases do not usually come to us with this comforting lack of ambiguity. That is why it is useful to think about ethical rules and ethical problems.

It may be helpful at this point to try to state a set of moral rules which attempt to do justice to the complexity of real cases—the possibility of conflicts, etc. Such a set of rules will look extremely complex and perhaps rather remote from real life. But this would be true, we must remember, of any attempt to make a reasonably complete verbal statement of how to carry out any familiar piece of behavior, for example, driving a car to the nearest grocery store and buying a quart of milk. The more watertight we try to make such a description, the more complex it gets. For example, before I back out of the driveway I check for approaching cars, people, animals, or objects back of the car, sounds of mechanical trouble in the car. None of these things may be in the forefront of my mind; my checking may be automatic and not consciously attended to. But if I am a good driver I will not pull out unless certain conditions prevail. And if I try to state these specifically, the description will be complex.

Here, then, is one attempt at a list of moral rules:

R 1. Do not harm persons, or perform actions which will probably harm persons, *except*

a. When the action is for the long-term good of the person(s) being harmed and is done with their consent where feasible.
b. When all other possible actions will cause greater harm to persons.
c. When the person has by his own free choice deserved to be harmed and the person doing the harm is the appropriate person to inflict this harm.
d. When an important obligation to make reparation to other persons or an extremely important commitment makes some harm or risk of harm to persons unavoidable. Occasionally relatively minor harm to persons may be justified by extraordinarily important obligations to benefactors or the opportunity to give extraordinary help to deserving persons.

R 2. If persons have been harmed, reparation must be made to them by the person responsible for harming them, *except*

a. When making reparation would involve greater harm to persons.

b. When the injured person with full knowledge and responsibility absolutely refuses reparation.

c. When the more important reparation, or an important commitment or an extremely important obligation to a benefactor is incompatible with making a less important reparation. Occasionally an extraordinarily important obligation to benefactors or opportunity to give extraordinary help to deserving or even undeserving persons may justify omitting relatively minor reparations.

R 3. Keep whatever commitments have been made *except*

a. When disproportionate harm would be done to persons by keeping the commitment or when an obligation to make reparation is incompatible with keeping the commitment.

b. When the person to whom the commitment applies, with full knowledge and responsibility releases the committed person from his commitment, or when the situation has changed to such an extent that the commitment has become pointless.

c. When a more important commitment, or an important obligation to a benefactor, or a very important obligation to be fair is incompatible with a less important commitment. Occasionally an extraordinary opportunity to help others, even if undeserving or even to benefit oneself, will justify nonfulfillment of a relatively minor commitment.

R 4. When a non-obligatory benefit is done to a person, that person must, if possible, return an otherwise non-obligatory benefit *except*

a. When this would cause harm to persons, conflict with an obligation to make reparation, or conflict with a more important commitment.

b. When the benefactor with full knowledge and responsibility absolutely refuses repayment.

c. When a more important obligation to repay benefits, or an important obligation to be fair, or a very important obligation to help others is incompatible with a less important obligation to repay benefits. Occasionally an extraordinarily important opportunity for self-improvement will justify omitting a relatively minor obligation to repay benefits.

R 5. Treat persons fairly, that is, purely on the basis of their merits *except*

a. When this would harm persons, conflict with an obligation to make reparation, conflict with a more important commitment, or conflict with a more important obligation to a benefactor.
b. When the person or persons involved with full knowledge and responsibility waive their right to be treated on their merits.
c. When a more important obligation of fairness, or an important benefit to others, or a very important benefit to oneself is incompatible with a less important obligation to be fair.

R 6. At some times, benefit persons who do not deserve these benefits under previous rules, *except*
a. When this would cause harm to persons, conflict with an obligation to make reparation, or with a commitment or with an obligation to repay benefits, or with an obligation at fairness.
b. When those who would be benefited with full knowledge and responsibility absolutely refuse the benefit.
c. When in every case where it was possible to benefit persons there was a more important obligation to self-improvement.

R 7. At some times perform actions which are likely to lead to moral or intellectual or self-improvement or greater happiness for oneself, *except*
a. When this would cause harm to others, or conflict with an obligation to make reparation, or with a commitment, or with an obligation to repay benefits, or with an obligation to fairness.
b. When the self-improving action, either in itself or because of its membership in a series of actions, would preclude ever benefiting other persons.
c. When the self-improving action would cause seriously greater harm to oneself.

There are probably other exceptions or qualifications needed in this list of rules, but this set is as complete as I can now make it. When we refer to this list of rules later on we will call them the *Revised Ranked Ross Rules*.

Note the *b* exception in R 2–R 6. This exception embodies a moral principle which seems to me to be obvious but which might be open to argument. The principle is that reparation, fulfillment of promises, repayment of benefits, and even fair treatment or benefits should not be forced on unwilling recipients. Obligations under rules R 2–R 6 give rights to persons, and the principle might also be restated as saying that persons can give up rights under these rules.

There is no exception of this kind for R 1; this embodies the moral principle that we cannot give up our right not to be killed, mutilated, etc. But note that consent can "extinguish" some kinds of harm; for example, if I freely give you title to all my goods you cannot then steal from me. There is also no "consent" exception to self-improvement; the very cases where someone is content to be miserable, ignorant, etc., are those in which self-improvement as a *moral* duty is most important.

R 1 needs a "lesser-evil" clause (clause *b*), but in R 2–R 6 conflicts with obligations under the same rule are dealt with in the *c* clauses. Exception *c* to R 1 embodies the moral view that a person can deserve to be harmed by way of punishment, but a nonretributivist could simply regard the condition as never fulfilled. The second part of the clause restricts punishment to those in some way authorized to inflict it, whoever those may be.

The *a* exception to R 1 authorizes harming someone for their own net good; obviously this exception should be invoked with great caution, and in case of doubt the refusal of consent by the person involved should be decisive. But obviously a doctor who amputates the foot of an unconscious man to get him clear of the debris of a collapsed building and thus save his life has not broken the moral prohibition against harming persons.

R 6 and R 7, being obligations to perform actions at *some* times, create special problems. In a given case a person may always have good reasons not to benefit others under R 6. For example, a person who needs all of his efforts merely to survive cannot be blamed for not lending others a helping hand. This situation is covered by exception *c* to R 6. Exception *b* to R 7 is an attempt to embody the principle that though in many cases one may put one's own welfare before benefiting nondeserving persons, if one *always* does so a moral fault has been committed. Finally, exception *c* to R 7 is an attempt to set out the intuition that though there is no obligation to choose the *most* self-improving action one can commit a moral fault by choosing limited goods for oneself which result in net harm. Some of these trickier clauses no doubt could be stated more clearly or precisely.

To what extent are these rules exhaustive, and to what extent are the exceptions exhaustive? I have tried to cover all relevant considerations, but I have undoubtedly failed. But I see no reason in principle why an exhaustive list of "obligation-making" characteristics of actions *cannot* be given, or a complete list of *kinds* of exceptions to moral rules cannot be given. This is not to say that each specific obligation-creating situation can be listed, or each specific exception-causing situation. But headings, fairly general but still specific enough to be informative, are another matter. And even an incomplete list can be useful: formal logic does not list every kind of valid argument but it lists enough to be very useful.

This list of moral rules may not resemble what you may be used to thinking of as a list of moral rules. But think about a familiar set of moral rules such as the Ten Commandments. There are commandments against theft and murder, which are ways of harming people, but not the only ways. Wounding someone or keeping someone illegally in prison are ways of harming people, but neither is mentioned specifically in the decalogue. Of course this does not mean that stabbing a man or locking him in a cellar are not wrong for a Jew or Christian who accepts the Ten Commandments. Harm of these kinds is considered as included under such commandments as "Thou shalt not kill."

Similarly, the decalogue enjoins honor to parents, and forbids adultery. These are important commitments but not the only kinds of commitment. We begin to see that the Ten Commandments mention *typical examples* of specific types of harm, commitment, and so on. Often more than one of our rules will apply to a specific commandment. For example, parents usually deserve our gratitude; theft is unfair as well as causing harm. Our rules R 1 to R 7 are an attempt to be more general than such specific commandments as "Thou shall not steal," which mentions only one type of harm. At the same time our list tries to be more specific and useful than very general rules, such as "Love your neighbor" or "Do as you would be done by."

Let us now return to situation ethics. We can see that many of the examples given by situationists are simply conflict of rules cases and that the intuitively appealing answers the situationists give to these dilemmas are exactly the answers which should be given on our set of rules. But this is not always true. Many later ethical writers, situationist and non-situationist, have been appalled at Fletcher's easy acceptance of atomic bombing, of sacrifice of human values in espionage and counterespionage.

In fact, a careful look at Fletcher's cases and the solutions he gives or hints at shows that sometimes Fletcher judges on a purely act-utilitarian basis, while in other cases he simply seems to express the ideas and preconceptions of an educated liberal of his age and background. This is not surprising, for if we attempt to use unaided moral intuition in each moral dilemma we are bound to be influenced by such factors as culture and environment.

Another drawback of Fletcher's position is that when he discusses the ultimate basis of morality he states that our moral systems rest ultimately on an unjustifiable decision—we simply posit a starting point and go on from there. This is, as Fletcher admits, a form of relativism. But as we saw in Chapter 1, the relativist cannot really take a firm objective stance about the rightness or wrongness of actions or principles. When Fletcher talks as if legalism were immoral, all he can really be saying is that legalism is immoral *if* you posit a situationist starting point. But it is equally true that if you posit a legalistic starting point, situationism is immoral.

Thus, situation ethics is a curious hodgepodge. It includes a legitimate protest against legalism and an illegitimate confusion of all rule-based ethics with legalism. It includes a relativist component and also an "ideal act-utilitarian" component. Therefore situation ethics is open to a great many of the objections made against relativism and utilitarianism earlier in this book.

The advantage of situation ethics is that it makes us ask ourselves whether any moral rule, especially a highly specific rule such as "Do not steal," is unbreakable. When we realize that the answer to this is probably "no," then we seem at first to be left to the mercies of unaided intuition, which can be confused by factors such as culture and environment.

From this dilemma a reasonable rule view can save us. A modified Ross Rule view like the one outlined in this chapter and the previous one can admit that no moral rule is absolutely unbreakable. But by limiting the kinds of considerations which can justify breaking a moral rule, a modified Rossian view keeps its ties with objectivity. Lying, for instance, is *prima facie* wrong. (Most Rossians argue that using language commits us to truth-telling.) If there are no overriding obligations, we can say with confidence that a given lie is morally wrong. But we are not forced to say with Kant that we must tell the truth even to a madman looking for his enemy. Given the forced choice between lying and causing harm to innocent persons, we can grant that lying is in that case allowable. But the choice must really be forced, and the bad consequences to be avoided by the lie must be of a certain kind. The rules we have given cannot, for example, be twisted to permit lying for our own advantage.

At this point you may wonder if there is any room for the individual conscience. Doesn't reducing morality to a set of complex rules make moral decision-making mechanical? But to ask this is to misunderstand what makes a decision mechanical. A judge, or for that matter an umpire or referee in sports, makes decisions within a framework of rules (rules in most cases far more complex than those given above). But the judge must decide which rules apply to a given case and just how those rules apply. Such decisions are not arbitrary; they involve consideration of reasons. But neither are such decisions mechanical. They involve judgment and, at least in unfamiliar types of cases, a certain amount of creativity.

Some people seem to think that the conscience can be completely nonmechanical only if it is completely creative, not tied down to any rules whatever. For them, the proper analogy for conscience is not the analogy of a judge applying the law, or an umpire applying rules, but rather the analogy of an artist creating a picture or a composer creating a piece of music. Just as to some a work of art is good if it expresses the personality of the artist, so some people want to say that a moral decision is good if it expresses the personality of the person making the decision. (This seems to be what some existentialists mean by a moral decision being judged by whether or not it is "authentic.")

But if, as we argued above, morality is based on a basic human nature and on the satisfaction of basic human social and personal needs, then morality cannot be purely creative in this way. Just as we cannot meet our needs for food or water or warmth by deciding to eat rocks or drink gasoline or cuddle up to a block of ice, so we cannot satisfy our social and personal needs by just any moral decision. Our moral decisions must take place within a framework fixed by our nature. (Of course, the existentialist and situationist try to deny this, but whether they can support this denial is another question.)

However, just as there is tremendous variety in the ways in which we can satisfy our physical needs, so there is considerable variety in the ways in which we can satisfy our social and personal needs by moral behavior. Especially within the categories of self-development and help to others, we can use considerable imagination and creativity. A specific commitment or an obligation not to cause harm may leave less scope for individuality, of course, just as in the realm of physical needs there is little variation possible in breathing or elimination of waste products.

The traditional view of conscience is that it is "practical reason," reason applying rules to specific situations. But to apply a rule requires judgment; we cannot give a rule for how to apply rules. If we needed rules to apply rules, then an endless regress would be generated.

Applying rules requires decisions as to matters of fact (e.g., "Who will be harmed if I do this?"), decisions as to degree of importance (e.g., "Is this an important promise?"), decisions as to which rule a case comes under (e.g., "Is only simple fairness involved here or do reparations for past injuries come into it?"). None of these decisions can be made mechanically. But that does not mean that the decisions are arbitrary, any more than the fact that a judge needs to make nonmechanical decisions means that his decisions are arbitrary.

Another way of expressing this point is to say that rules of the sort we find in law or in mortality need to be *interpreted*, not just (mechanically) *applied*. Conscience *interprets* the moral law. This will involve drawing out the *implications* of rules—but implications in a fairly wide sense, not just the logical implications of a law. For example, we may have always been willing to agree that people should be treated fairly. But we may not always have realized that certain kinds of sexual stereotyping could lead to unfair treatment. Certain habits of thought about "men's work" and "women's work," or certain preconceived ideas about "womanliness" or "manliness" may have resulted in unfair treatment to both men and women.

The general principle of fairness is clear enough: we should disregard irrelevant differences in making decisions about things like jobs, pay, and the like. But just what differences are irrelevant? To decide this requires judgment, and no complete set of rules can be given to guide this judgment. This does not mean that the judgments will be arbitrary, however. Our judgment will be guided by analogies with past cases, by arguments put forward by one side or the other. But eventually we will have to arrive at a decision on the basis of these analogies or these arguments. Again, there is a close connection with the process by which a judge reaches decisions, especially in "common law" or "equity" cases, where the judge has to apply precedents and consider arguments given by both sides. Such judgment is not arbitrary; it is in one sense not "creative." But it is not mechanical either: we cannot replace judges by computers.

In the remainder of this book we will try to apply the rule view which we have been discussing to some troublesome moral problems. Where appropriate we will also say something about the solutions to these problems which might be given by an egoist or a utilitarian or a situationist. But in most cases there is no general solution to a problem such as abortion or euthanasia or war within any of these theories. An egoist, for instance, will permit abortion if it is to his advantage, forbid it if it is not. He has no *general* position. A Ranked Ross rule view, on the other hand, can at least attempt a solution in principle to moral dilemmas and give us help in dealing with particular cases. Indeed, a very important argument for a "neo-Rossian" or "hierarchical rule" view in ethics is that it does permit us to *argue* about ethical problems, to treat them rationally and not just emotionally.

DISCUSSION QUESTIONS

1. What point might the Reverend Butler have wanted to make about Christ and the rich young man? (Matthew 19:16-26)

2. Do you think that some situations might justify lying? If so, what kind of situation? Be specific. If not, why not?

3. Answer the same questions as in 2, for stealing.

4. Answer the same questions as in 2, for adultery.

5. Answer the same questions as in 2, for taking a human life.

6. Give some instances of moral conflict. Do such instances create a problem for the situationist?

7. Try to find a case where the set of ethical rules given in this chapter seems to conflict with your own moral intuition. State the case clearly.

8. Take an apparent conflict between the Revised Ranked Ross Rules and moral intuition. See if you can find a way of resolving the apparent conflict. If it cannot be resolved, how might the rules be modified to take care of this case?

9. Could the Revised Rank Ross Rules provide a workable code of ethics for everyday living? Why or why not?

10. Apply the Revised Ranked Ross Rules to the cases discussed by the Reverends Butler and Crozier. What should have been done in these cases according to the rules? What further information would you need?

FURTHER READINGS

EWING, A. C., *Ethics*, pp. 61-77. New York: The Free Press, 1953.

FLETCHER, JOSEPH, *Situation Ethics, the New Morality*. Philadelphia: Westminster Press, 1966.

FRANKENA, WILLIAM, *Ethics* (2nd ed.). pp. 43-61. Englewood Cliffs, N.J.: Prentice-Hall, Inc., 1973.

FRANKENA, WILLIAM, and JOHN GRANROSE, *Introductory Readings in Ethics*. Englewood Cliffs, N.J.: Prentice-Hall, Inc., 1974:

CARRITT, E. F., "Moral Rules," pp. 72-73.

MAYO, BERNARD, "Criticisms of Act-Deontologism," pp. 75–79.

RASHDALL, HASTINGS, "Criticisms of Act-Deontologism," pp. 74-75.

SIDGWICK, HENRY, "Criticisms of Act-Deontologism," pp. 73-74.

SELLARS, WILFRED, and JOHN HOSPERS, *Readings in Ethical Theory* (2nd ed.). New York: Appleton-Century-Crofts, 1970:

PRICHARD, H. A., "Does Moral Philosophy Rest on a Mistake?" pp. 86-97.

6 The Sanctity of Life: At What Price?

Mrs. Fothringay lay in the big hospital bed, her worn face hardly less white than the pillowcase. But there was a discreet touch of color on her lips and her hair and nails were as beautifully tended as ever. She seemed to be asleep, but despite the quiet with which Dr. Buchan eased his bulky body into the room she opened her eyes as he came to the bedside. "Sit down somewhere where I can see you, Doctor," she said, in the voice of a woman used to having her way. "This isn't a medical call, Doctor. I want to talk to you about some things which might affect my decision to leave my money to your hospital. I presume the amount involved is enough to give you a certain patience with some impertinent questions."

Dr. Buchan smiled. "I've known you a long time Mrs. Fothringay. You don't have to brandish your money to make me come and talk to you."

The old woman pursed her lips. "I don't just want to chat, Doctor. I'd like to get your answer to some questions about things that go on in this hospital. Next door there is Sarah Kennedy. She hasn't been conscious for weeks and probably won't ever be conscious again. She might as well be dead but you won't let her die. You're spending heaven knows how much money to keep her alive, if you can call it alive. Yet, at the same time, the nurses tell me that hundreds of abortions are being performed in this hospital, some of them so close to term that if the fetuses were treated as premature babies and promptly put in incubators they might survive."

Dr. Buchan frowned. "I don't see any parallel, Mrs. Fothringay," he snapped. "Mrs. Kennedy is a human being, with a right to live. The women who are having the abortions have rights, too, under the laws of this state."

Mrs. Fothringay lifted herself slightly from the pillows in her excitement. "And what about the babies?"

Dr. Buchan pressed her shoulder gently to make her lie back. "There are no babies involved, Mrs. Fothringay," he said soothingly. "The fetus can't be considered a person. An abortion is a surgical procedure for the removal of unwanted tissue, no different in principle from the removal of a cancer or an appendix."

Mrs. Fothringay's eyes snapped. "I won't argue with you about whether a fetus is a person, although I don't see what standards you could use to deny personhood to a fetus that wouldn't apply to Mrs. Kennedy. She is as unable to see or hear or think or act as they are, and she's as dependent on your machines to survive as the fetus is on its mother. But whether or not the fetus is a person, whether or not you want to call it a baby, you can't compare it with a cancer or an appendix. A fetus will grow into a human being if it's not interfered with; an appendix or a cancer won't."

Dr. Buchan wrinkled his brow in puzzlement. "I don't see what you expect of me, Mrs. Fothringay. The laws allow abortions, and most doctors who aren't Roman Catholics feel that abortion is justified. And I'm not sure what your point is about Mrs. Kennedy. I thought she was a friend of yours."

There were tears in Mrs. Fothringay's eyes but her voice was under control. "It's precisely because I'm a friend of Sarah's that I don't like to see her body kept alive when her personality has gone for good. Nor do I expect you to resist the present abortion laws, especially if you yourself feel that they're justified. What I did hope to get from you was some expression of principle, some *reason* for the things I've mentioned. Is letting an aborted fetus die when medicine could save it very different from letting a full-term baby die because it has deformities or an incurable disease? And is that very different from exposing unwanted babies as some cultures did? Where do you draw the line?"

Dr. Buchan stood up. "Mrs. Fothringay, you're exciting yourself. I'm a hospital administrator, not an expert on medical ethics. What the law allows and my professional colleagues approve is what I go by. If the law changes or medical opinion changes, my policies will change."

Mrs. Fothringay closed her eyes and her voice was remote. "Thank you, Doctor. I think you've told me what I want to know. You've said nothing that a doctor in Nazi Germany couldn't have said. If our government starts sterilizing those they consider unfit, or using charity patients for medical experiments, I'm sure your hospital will be available—if the law allows and your colleagues approve. But my money won't be available. I think I'll try to put it in the hands of someone with a bit more principle."

Dr. Buchan's face was red, but he tried to make his voice calm and soothing. "I'm sorry about that, Mrs. Fothringay. We could have used your money but I'm sure you'll put it to some good use. I don't worry too much about principles—I'm a practical man. But I did tell you the truth."

"That wasn't very practical in this instance, Doctor. Perhaps you've a few lurking principles, after all." She turned her face away and after a moment Dr. Buchan slipped out in the corridor, shaking his head.

Our story raises two issues which are currently being debated in our society: abortion and euthanasia. Both controversies raise two questions: "What is a person?" and "Can persons be killed under some circumstances?" If the fetus is not yet a person, then abortion is not killing a person but rather killing a possible person or preventing a person. If a patient who is being kept alive only by artificial means is no longer a person, then turning off the machines is not killing a person. On the other hand, if a fetus *is* a person, abortion is the killing of a person and could be justified, if at all, only by a certainty that every possible alternative would cause greater harm. Similarly, if a person being kept alive by artificial means is still a person, then an action that caused the death of that person would seem to be the killing of a person.

In many ways we have expanded our idea of what a person is throughout history. Very primitive tribes do not seem to regard anyone outside the tribe as "really people," and even a civilized culture like that of ancient China sometimes regarded non-Chinese as "devils" rather than as people. In slave-owning cultures slaves are not regarded as persons; even some of the Greek and Roman philosophers regarded them as merely "living tools." Some cultures, and even some religious groups, have regarded women as less than persons. One major reason for change in these attitudes was the rise of Christianity. Christians insisted that all humans have souls, that Christ died for everyone. This meant that all were children of God and should be treated accordingly. At first Christianity did not try to change the legal institution of slavery. St. Paul, for example, sent a Christian runaway slave back to his Christian master. But he insisted that the master treat the slave as "a most dear brother." This attitude eventually meant the end of slavery, for if you regard the slave as a person, slavery as an institution becomes unworkable.

Opponents of abortion are often traditional Christians who believe that the human person is a union of soul and body and that soul and body are united at the moment of conception. Thus the killing of a fetus is the killing of a person, in their view. This group usually believes that the soul and body are united so long as the body is alive, and thus they oppose euthanasia if it involves direct killing. Some members of this group would allow letting a person die if there is no hope of recovery and only extraordinary artificial means will sustain life. Mrs. Fothringay in our story could be in this position since she seems to object to abortion but be in favor of letting Mrs. Kennedy die.

Many nowadays do not share the traditional belief that the person is soul and body, or do not believe that the soul is united to the body at conception or is separated from the body only at complete stopping of all bodily functions. These people, in order to arrive at a reasonable judgment about abortion or euthanasia, must think out their own standards as to what a person is.

This is not as easy to do as it might seem. If ability to function fully at an adult human level is to be the standard of personhood, then children would not be persons, nor would many people who suffer from mental disorders or from physical disorders that affect brain functioning. If we try to include children by saying that *future* functioning at full adult capacity is the standard, then we seem to eliminate some very old or very ill persons whose abilities are slowly declining from this level. At the same time it is hard to see how the difference between a young child, a baby, and a fetus is more than a matter of degree if future potential is our standard. If we try to save the personhood of old or ill persons by making *past* functioning at an adult level part of our standard, children are eliminated again. If we try to eliminate the fetus by making present self-awareness or conscious knowledge and choice the standard, then very young babies might be eliminated, as well as sick people in protracted comas.

It might be possible to get some complicated set of criteria which would specify as persons just those entities whom the majority of our society seems currently inclined to treat as persons, but such a set of criteria would be likely to be completely *ad hoc* and arbitrary. If public opinion changed, there would seem no reason not to change the criteria. And public hysteria or government propaganda can certainly change attitudes. Children in Nazi Germany were systematically taught that Jews, gypsies, and mentally defective people were "subhuman" and had no rights.

To illustrate this point, imagine that some mutation in the human stock led to the birth of babies who varied a great deal from the human norm. Perhaps, as in A.E. Van Vogt's science fiction novel *Slan!*, they had two hearts, golden tendrils in their hair, and telepathic abilities. Fear and insecurity might very well lead to hysteria; such children might be labeled "monsters" and killed or denied human rights. To stay with science fiction for a moment, suppose we meet intelligent beings on other planets. By what standards will we decide whether these are to be treated as we treat human persons? Again, if super-computers began to act in a human way, as in some of Robert Heinlein's novels, would we have to give them human rights?

Once we began thinking about such examples we realize that our idea of what makes a person depends a good deal on habit and custom. Those who for one reason or another cannot assert their rights as persons often find those rights disregarded and find themselves regarded as less than persons. Opponents of abortion argue that this is just what has happened in the case of the fetus. Opponents of euthanasia fear that euthanasia laws which allow letting a person die rather than keeping him alive by extraordinary means will lead to a policy of killing persons whom society finds inconvenient. Both might agree that any permitted killing or allowing of death weakens respect for human life.

Others might carry this argument further. Those who oppose capital punishment would argue that for the state to use the death penalty weakens respect for life. Pacifists argue that killing in war is never justified. This raises the questions: "Is killing another person ever morally justified? If so, under what circumstances?" The two cases where many people would be willing to allow killing are *in defense of self or others*, and *as a punishment for a serious crime.*

Consider defensive killing first. Suppose someone is trying to kill an innocent person and the *only* way to stop him is by killing *him.* Consider, for example, a case where Rose refuses to marry Vincent because he mocks her religion. He nurses his resentment and blames her church for her refusal. One day Vincent appears on a balcony in Rose's parish church with a machine gun, swearing to kill every member of the congregation. His first burst narrowly misses a mother and child and wounds an old lady. A quick-witted member of the congregation sees that a pull at a nearby rope will bring down a heavy window frame on Vincent's head, stopping him from killing others but probably killing Vincent. Should he pull the rope or should he stand there and let the congregation be mowed down?

A great many of us would say that in that case it would be better to stop the gunman, even at the price of killing him, rather than permit the pointless slaughter of the whole congregation. If Vincent had killed the woman and child instead of just missing them, we might have even less hesitation, for if death is ever justifiable as a punishment it would surely be in a case where the criminal has himself killed others. But even if Vincent were insane and not legally or morally responsible for his actions, it might be justifiable to kill him in order to save the congregation.

In this case, as in many others, we are faced with a choice between evils. It is a bad thing to kill Vincent, even if he has killed others. But it is an even worse thing to stand by and let Vincent slaughter innocent men, women, and children. If these are *really* the only two choices, isn't it right to choose the lesser evil? It can be argued in a similar way that killing in war is sometimes the lesser evil, though this may be open to dispute in particular cases.

It is certainly true that people will try to abuse "lesser evil" arguments. A wife murderer may argue, "Killing my wife was a lesser evil than living with her." But of course any argument can be twisted, and in the cases where an argument is being misused no impartial person would concede that the alleged lesser evil *was* the least evil of possible choices. For example, to the wife murderer an impartial person might say: "In what way is this the lesser evil? From whom? Even leaving out of consideration your wife's rights, is it better for you to be a murderer than an unhappy husband? Is it really the *only* alternative? What about separation? Divorce? Even desertion?" But in the case of the man with the machine gun it might be that his death was the only alternative to massacre, and many impartial persons would grant that it was the lesser evil.

War, of course, is a much more complex issue than simple self-defense or defense of others. In an effort to set reasonable restrictions on cases where war, and killing in war, might be justified, some philosophers have arrived at lists of conditions for a "just war," such as the following: Nation A is justified in waging war with Nation B if and only if: (*a*) Nation A has been attacked by Nation B or is going to the aid of Nation C, which has been attacked by Nation B. (*b*) The war has been legally declared by the properly constituted authorities of Nation A. (*c*) The intentions of Nation A in waging the war are confined to repelling the attack by Nation B and establishing a peace that is fair to all. (*d*) Nation A has a reasonable hope of success in repelling the attack and establishing a just peace. (*e*) Nation A cannot secure these ends without waging war; it has considered or tried all other means and is waging war only as a last resort. (*f*) The good done by Nation A's waging war against Nation B can reasonably be expected to outweigh the evil done by their waging war. (*g*) Nation A does not use or anticipate using any means of waging war which are themselves immoral, e.g., the avoidable killing of innocent persons.

I think it would be useful to examine the way in which reasonable men do in fact use such criteria in arguing about the justification of particular wars. We will begin with some of the simpler and less restrictive criteria and then go on to the more complex and arguable cases. Probably the least restrictive criterion is *b*, the condition that war be legally declared by constituted authority. However, to see that this criterion is still used in current debates on the justifiability of particular wars, we need only consider the criticism made by critics of President Johnson's actions in committing American forces to a war in Vietnam without a declaration of war by Congress. Here the legality of the action was in question, not Johnson's position as a duly constituted authority. Nor was the criterion itself rejected by defenders of the administration; the attempt was made to argue that the Gulf of Tonkin resolution gave authority for the commitment of troops. Again, critics of the war both in this country and abroad criticized the Thieu government as not being a duly constituted authority, and defenders of the war attempted to establish Thieu as the duly constituted authority on the basis of elections. The criterion, at any rate, seemed to be recognized by both parties as relevant.

Condition *a* is somewhat more complex. Obviously, "they attacked first" has been widely used as a defense of the justice of a war, and is so used today. That the Confederates fired on Fort Sumter, that Hitler invaded Poland, that the Japanese attacked Pearl Harbor, that the United States invaded at the Bay of Pigs, has in each case given the attacked people a firm conviction of the rightness of their cause. The Korean conflict caused nothing like the anguish created by the Vietnamese war in the minds of Americans, because there seemed to be a clear invasion across an established frontier. In the case of Vietnam, defenders of the war argued that a similar invasion occurred, and opponents of the war tried to establish that American support of Diem amounted to an attack on the legitimate authority in Vietnam. Thus, seemingly both accept the principle that he who strikes first is in the wrong. The actions of Israel in the Six Day War were attacked by some as a preemptive strike, and defended by others as a response to preparations and pressures amounting to an attack.

Condition *g* plunges us further into complexity. Those who used the My Lai massacre as a basis for an attack on the war (rather than merely condemning the incident itself) seemed to be arguing that the government intended or permitted or at least could have reasonably foreseen the inevitability of such incidents. Defenders of the war (not of the massacre itself) argued that the government neither intended nor condoned the incident and that such incidents could not be foreseen nor prevented by even the best-intentioned government. Again, nations that use weapons which do in fact cause the death of noncombatants frequently try to justify them on the basis that such deaths were the unintended result of actions taken against military targets. Where this justification is implausible, as in such cases as the fire-bombing of Dresden and Tokyo, the robot bombing of London, the atomic bomb drops in Japan, the use of anti-personnel weapons in the bombing of North Vietnam, and so on, the perpetrators are widely condemned by impartial persons.

Condition *c*, that the intentions of a nation attempting to justify a war are restricted to repelling attack and establishing a just peace, is a claim widely made—for example, by the U.S. government in the Vietnam war, by Israel in the two wars with the Arab nations, and by Biafra in the recent Nigerian war. Where some doubt is cast on such claims, as for example by Biafra's initial sally outside of Ibo territory, or by Israel's colonization of the Sinai, defenders of the country in question feel that the imputation of motives other than defense and just settlement is one which must be repelled.

Condition *d*, reasonable hope of success, has been used by recent critics of the Vietnam war and by critics of Biafra's continued struggle in the last stages of the war, and has undoubtedly influenced such events as Czechoslovakia's decision not to resist the Russian invasion militarily. Nor is the criterion denied by those against whom it is levied as an accusation; repeated claims of eventual victory are made, despite their implausibility.

For an example of Condition *e*, war only as a last resort, we might consider the "war" of the Nazis against the German Jews. If the complete "freeing" of Germany from Jewish influence was the desired end, then the recent example of Poland, which over the past few years has caused the emigration of most of its Jewish population by social and political pressures, shows that the use of violence was not the "last resort" in Germany. Despicable and horrible as the Polish tactic was, it secured the desired end without the use of violence and, ironically enough, more efficiently than Hitler's methods. Examples having to do with national conflicts are less easy to find, but one might cite the U.S. invasion of the Dominican Republic as a case where an accusation was made that the use of a military invasion was far from the last resort to secure the end desired, an allegation resisted by Johnson's defenders. At any rate, no one seems anxious to admit that they employed war or other violence as other than a last resort.

Finally, regarding Condition *f*, the claim is always made that the good done by waging a war outweighs the evil. Where it is seriously challenged, as in the destruction of Vietnam by the current conflict, or the starvation of Biafran children by the carrying on of the Biafran war, then this fact in itself often leads to the condemnation of a war judged just on other grounds. Just such considerations changed many Americans from hawks to doves or gave pause to early supporters of Biafra.

Now plainly, lying claims are often made that such criteria are met when in fact they are not, and passion and partiality often blind participants in a conflict to gross violations of such criteria. But every one of these criteria has been used in recent times to accuse warring governments of injustice, and to defend governments' claims to having justice on their side. No one is willing to admit to violation of these criteria; everyone is anxious to show that their actions conform to them. Nor is it impossible for reasonably impartial persons to discover whether these criteria are in fact satisfied in particular instances.

Those who claim to be reasonable and well-intentioned but who cannot accept pacifism have a special need of such criteria. The pure pacifist can condemn both sides in every war: he has no problems in this respect. But he is in practice ineffective, partly because men always have and perhaps always will make a distinction between Genghis Khan invading the peaceful village to pillage and rape, and the villagers who spring to their own defense (to choose an example safely remote).

Nonpacifists hearing of a border war between China and India, a rebellion in Biafra based on fear of genocide, an invasion in Hungary or Cuba or Czechoslovakia, must make up their minds about these events. No doubt it would be best if all conflicts ceased. But unless and until they do, we are forced to take sides, and in taking sides we are forced to use some standards.

The most frequent standard other than those in the traditional just-war criteria listed previously is simply some version of "the righteousness of our cause." Because we are Communists (or anti-Communists), because we are white (or black), because we have the true belief which will save the world, we may war on our opponents, using any means, disregarding any standards. It is this sort of position which is dangerous to the peace of the world. If every nation observed the traditional criteria of the just war, wars would be infrequent, short, and relatively limited.

But, it may be argued, in modern nuclear warfare it is impossible in practice to observe these criteria. Just so, and a recognition of this fact on the part of the great powers may be partly responsible for keeping our uneasy peace. True, there is a "balance of terror," but there are situations in which moral considerations and fear of world reaction have played a greater part than fear of retaliation. Arguably the position of the United States before Russia had effective atomic armaments, and the position of Russia with regard to China at the present time, are cases of this kind.

Some critics of the just-war theory point out that the theory has often been used to justify policies which seem to be obviously immoral, such as the saturation bombing of cities or the use of germ warfare on whole populations. But of course any theory can be twisted or distorted by partisans, and obviously such tactics are, on the face of it, contrary to such principles as *f* and *g* above. It may be the casuists can attempt justification of such actions on the basis of the just-war theory, but the "righteous cause" theory can justify such actions without any acrobatics.

Another criticism is that just-war theory is immoral in attempting to show that under some circumstances it would be "just" to perform immoral acts and to contribute to evil consequences. But of course this is not the position of the just-war theorist, nor of the ordinary nonpacifist criticizing some particular war. Neither would admit that self-defense is immoral, nor that inflicting damage on an aggressor who is attempting to destroy you is an unambiguously evil consequence. Even if certain consequences of war are taken to be clearly evil, any mature morality must make room for cases in which we must choose the lesser of two evils.

It is not my intention to defend war as an instrument of national policy, or to justify any particular war. In fact, I believe that certain modern wars have been justified, but a consistent defender of the just-war theory might very well feel that modern wars inevitably violate the traditional just-war criteria. However, I think that the cause of peace is not well served by the rejection of the just-war theory, leaving us in practice with the choice between pacifism and the "righteous cause" type of justification. As I have tried to show, the traditional criteria for just war can be regarded as an explication of the standards which are used by many people of good will to criticize actual wars. Of course for the pure pacifist, any attempt to justify or defend any war will be morally monstrous. But this position is by no means an obviously true one, and it must be justified on its own merits.

Having discussed war at some length, we can now deal more briefly with capital punishment. Obviously, some of the same questions that apply to a just war apply to justifying capital punishment: It is the last resort, or are there other means of reaching the same result? Does it do more good than harm? Is the execution decreed by the legal authorities? Is the execution humane, not causing unnecessary suffering to the criminal? Reasonable hope of success is hardly ever a problem; and the idea of a peace fair to all doesn't seem to apply, but we *can* ask whether the legal authorities are confining their intentions to the proper end of punishment and not trying to secure some political end by the execution.

It is the first condition that will be different in the case of capital punishment; the state does not execute a murderer in self-defense, not, at least, if "self-defense" is meant in any ordinary way. In an extended sense the state may be said to act in self-defense in that it acts in defense of its members. Certainly it can be said that the criminal "started it," that the criminal is the aggressor and the state the defender.

I suspect that the execution of a criminal especially troubles our consciences for several reasons. First, an execution is something done "in cold blood" with deliberation and forethought. In wartime our emotions are aroused; it is easy to feel that we are being forced to retaliate. But a legal execution with its elaborate judicial procedure, its long delays, its appointed day of execution, has a chilling sort of deliberateness about it. It is clear that at many stages of the proceedings we could stop and refrain from killing the criminal. A condemned criminal knows that he will be killed and knows that society could refrain from killing him. Some opponents of capital punishment have argued that a death penalty is in itself cruel and inhumane, partly because of the effect of this knowledge on the criminal. There is some evidence, too, that executions cause harrowing emotions in other prisoners, in prison guards and officials, and even in judges and elected officials who must pass death sentences.

Another factor that makes us uneasy about capital punishment is the feeling, whether justified or not, that if the state deliberately takes life, then private individuals will feel less reluctance to take life. It is argued that if the state holds life sacred, others are encouraged to hold life sacred, whereas if the state kills for its ends, the citizens of the state will feel more justified in killing to attain their ends.

A factor in many people's attitude toward capital punishment is their religious belief or unbelief. When almost everyone believed that human beings were judged by God and rewarded or punished after death, few people objected to capital punishment. After all, if an innocent man was executed God would judge him after death and recompense him. And a guilty man faced with death might repent and save his soul. But in the present-day atmosphere of greater unbelief and less confident belief, more people regard death as total extinction. Thus life becomes more precious. If an innocent man is executed, nothing can make it up to him, and whether a condemned criminal repents or not is unimportant since he has no immortal soul to save. This explains the fact, which some have found puzzling or scandalous, that religious believers are more likely than agnostics or atheists to support capital punishment.

However, not all justifications for capital punishment are connected with religious belief. An argument which has weight with many people is that a criminal already condemned to life imprisonment has nothing to lose by killing a fellow inmate or a prison guard. Again, many people feel that if the criminal is able to kill and the state cannot retaliate with the threat of a death penalty, the state is put at a relative disadvantage. Indeed, a good deal of agitation for the restoration of the death penalty is based on the belief that execution is the ultimate threat or deterrent, and that high crime rates would be lowered.

The issues on both sides are in need of further discussion. Often the opponents of the death penalty seem to beg the question by assuming that the death penalty as imposed by the state is somehow the same sort of thing as murder committed by a private person. This might be true, but it needs argument. Presumably most people would reject the idea that when the state takes money from its citizens by taxation this encourages robbery or extortion. They would reject this idea because they see an important difference between taxation and robbery or extortion. And it is arguable that there is as great a difference between legal execution and murder as there is between taxation and robbery.

On the other side of the question the feeling that a death penalty is an effective deterrent does not seem to be supported by statistical evidence. It is true that the available evidence is probably inadequate and that many statistical arguments against the death penalty are bad ones. But the feeling of many people that the death penalty *must* be an effective deterrent seems to be based on their own reactions rather than on objective evidence; they feel that *they* would be deterred by a death penalty, so others would be too.

In view of the uncertainties about the pros and cons of the death penalty, it might seem that the humane course would be to oppose capital punishment. But if society has the right to kill in self-defense in a defensive war, surely it can kill in "self-defense" against criminals who take the lives of innocent people.

In summary, then, there are a number of cases in which some responsible people believe they can justify taking human life. Abortion, euthanasia, war, and capital punishment are among them. In some of these cases, especially abortion, the question of whether the life we are taking is to be regarded as the life of a person is a crucial one. In other cases, considerations of defense, of guilt, and so on, apply. The taking of any life lightly or wantonly, even animal life, would seem to be immoral, but morally sensitive people of good will can see some situations in which the taking of life may be justified. To kill may be always on the face of it evil, but it may sometimes be the lesser evil.

DISCUSSION QUESTIONS

1. Apply the just-war conditions, insofar as you can, to the case of abortion. Which conditions seem to apply? How? What conclusion would this lead you to? What other factors are relevant?
2. Answer Question 1, substituting enthanasia for abortion.
3. What factors other than those mentioned in the chapter should be considered in deciding whether capital punishment is justified?
4. Aside from the criminal himself, who should be considered in sentencing a murderer? Should the victim's family and their feelings be considered? The murderer's family and their feelings?
5. How would your opinion on abortion be affected if one parent wanted the baby? Is it relevant whether the parents are married?
6. Can we distinguish between killing someone and letting him die? How? Would there be borderline cases?
7. Read some pro- or anti-abortion literature. What arguments are given? How good are the arguments? Do the same for literature for or against euthanasia.
8. Consider a particular war in terms of the just-war criteria. Is this war justified in terms of those criteria or not?
9. Prepare an argument for or against capital punishment, trying to answer objections from the other side.
10. What arguments could Dr. Buchan have used in replying to Mrs. Fothringay? How might she have replied?

FURTHER READINGS

Beauchamp, Thomas, *Ethics and Public Policy*, Parts 2, 3, 6, and 7. Englewood Cliffs, N.J.: Prentice-Hall, Inc., 1975:

Bedau, Hugo Adam, "Deterrence and the Death Penalty: A Reconsideration," pp. 106-122.

Flew, Antony, "The Principle of Euthanasia," pp. 409-424.

Purtill, Richard L., "On the Just War," pp. 190-195.

RESCHER, NICHOLAS, "The Allocation of Exotic Medical Lifesaving Therapy," pp. 425-440.

VAN DER HAAG, ERNEST, "On Deterrence and the Death Penalty," pp. 94–105.

WELLS, DONALD, "How Much Can 'The Just War' Justify?" pp. 180-189.

RACHELS, JAMES, *Moral Problems* (2nd ed.), Parts 2, 6, and 7. New York: Harper & Row, 1975:

ANSCOMBE, G.E.M., "War and Murder," pp 285-297.

BRANDT, RICHARD, "The Morality and Rationality of Suicide." pp. 363-387.

HOLLAND, R. F., "Suicide," pp. 388-400.

NARVESON, JAN, "Pacifism: A Philosophical Analysis," pp. 346-360.

RAMSEY, PAUL, "The Morality of Abortion," pp. 37-58.

THOMSON, JUDITH JARVIS, "A Defense of Abortion," pp. 59-70.

WASSERSTROM, RICHARD, *Today's Moral Problems*, Parts 2 and 7. New York: the Macmillan Company, 1975:

GRISEZ, GERMAIN, "Abortion: Ethical Arguments," pp. 83-103.

HART, H.L.A., "Prolegomenon to the Principles of Punishment," pp. 272-291.

MORRIS, HERBERT, "Persons and Punishment," pp. 302-323.

REGAN, TOM, "A Defense of Pacifism," pp. 452-464.

WARREN, MARY ANNE, "On the Moral and Legal Status of Abortion," pp. 120-135.

WASSERSTROM, "The Laws of War," pp. 482-496.

7 Sexual Morality: Personal Relations

Laurie stared at her rapidly cooling coffee as she absentmindedly picked at the polish on her nails. She had a real problem, and no idea of how to solve it. She had just lost her roommate, Sylvia, who had moved to San Francisco for a new job. Laurie's boyfriend, Steve, had told her not to look for another roommate: he'd move and they could live together "so we can see how we get along." He hadn't come right out and said he'd marry her if they "got along," but he'd hinted at it. Laurie loved Steve and didn't want to lose him. Should she say no, and maybe lose him? Or should she say yes—and maybe lose him later anyway?

It wasn't as if she hadn't had plenty of advice about things like this. Myrna at the beauty shop had taken Laurie under her wing when she found out that Laurie had just move to the city from a small farming town. *Her* opinion was very positive. "Men just want one thing. Don't give it away—make them marry you for it." Laurie frowned. That seemed cold-blooded and mercenary; an attitude like that couldn't be right. At the other extreme was Dr. Norris, the minister of her home-town church. He'd talked to her a long time about the Christian ideal of marriage and how loving a husband and children was a preparation for loving God.

But at the end he looked at her rather sadly and said: "Laurie, I don't really feel that what I've said means much to you because I don't really feel that you're a committed Christian. Perhaps you'll come to be one as you live and learn. But remember this—a man who really loves you won't use you. He'll offer you his commitment; he'll want to give more than he wants to get. Keep that in mind when you're alone in the city."

Laurie had been impressed, but Dr. Norris was right; religion didn't really mean all that much to her. And as for commitment, she wasn't really sure she was ready for it herself. Maybe she'd be "using" Steve as much as he'd be "using" her—to learn and explore. And what would be wrong with that? But then there were her mother and father, and she knew how Mother would feel, and she knew what Dad would say, and . . . Laurie shook her head. She had to get back to work; she'd stretched the coffee break too long already. But *what* was she going to tell Steve tonight?

Not too many years ago Laurie's problem would have been a rather different one. Living with Steve would have been very likely to lead to an illegitimate child, and the social pressures against living together without marriage and against illegitimacy were both extremely severe. Steve's proposition would have been unfair to Laurie in obvious ways, since the social pressures on him would be less and he could have left Laurie quite literally holding the baby.

But at present, improved methods of birth control make pregnancy unlikely and society speaks with a divided voice. Fewer people have strong religious convictions which prevent them from engaging in premarital sexual intimacy. Living together without marriage is no longer obviously unwise or obviously unjust. So the question now becomes, "Are there any remaining moral reasons against (or for) Steve's proposition?"

As we saw in the first part of the book, the ethical relativist can give no answers to such questions, and the egoist or act utilitarian can give no general answers. The egoist can answer only in terms of what is beneficial to him, the act utilitarian can only calculate whether this particular act will cause more good on the whole than other acts available to him. But a rule utilitarian can ask whether there should be rules about sexual conduct, and if so what rules would be for the greatest good of the greatest number. A supporter of a rule theory of ethics, such as the Rossian view, can ask whether certain kinds of sexual behavior violates the rules he supports.

Consider the Rossian point of view on sexual ethics. Some kinds of sexual behavior, such as rape, are obviously ways of harming another person and are forbidden by the rule against harming persons. Other kinds of behavior, such as unfaithfulness to a marriage partner, obviously violate commitments. Seduction by lying or false promises violates other sorts of commitments. Promiscuous relationships without affection are almost certainly harmful to personal development and therefore violate the rule commanding self-improvement. But what about affectionate, long-lasting relationships freely entered into on both sides but without that formal commitment we call marriage? What, in other words (giving the boyfriend the benefit of the doubt), of the arrangement that Steve proposed to Laurie?

Of course Steve may be planning to exploit Laurie, to "love her and leave her." His hints at marriage may be mere bait, his intention to get what he can from Laurie with no concern for her welfare.

But suppose that Steve, like Laurie, is sincerely in love but not really sure that he is ready for a total commitment. Suppose that there is no deceit or exploitation on either side. Is there then anything wrong with Steve and Laurie living together and having sexual relations without marriage? Many couples doing just that would claim that they are hurting no one and breaking no commitments to anyone. If these claims are true why is what they are doing considered wrong by many people?

In our society the major reason sexual relationships of this kind are considered wrong is the influence of the Judeo-Christian ideal of marriage as a total and exclusive commitment. The traditional Judeo-Christian view is that marriage partners should not only be faithful to each other during marriage, but that they should be *prospectively* faithful—"save themselves" for their eventual husband or wife by refraining from premarital sexual relationships. This view is based on the idea of marriage as the most important purely human relationship and the family as the most important purely human institution. On this view the total commitment of husband and wife to each other and to their children is both a preparation for and a foretaste of the total commitment of the human soul to God. Like that commitment, marriage must be total and exclusive (and, on the traditional view, lifelong).

Perhaps only a minority of people in our society now hold this traditional view of marriage. Even when it was theoretically accepted by the majority it was rarely practiced to the full. The so-called "double standard" held that saving oneself for marriage was much more important for the bride than for the groom—an idea which the purely religious view has no room for. Purely pagan or pragmatic considerations influenced this watering down of the Judeo-Christian view—the idea of women as property rather than persons, the importance placed on "pure" lines of descent, and so on.

But of course many people in our society do not hold even a corrupt or watered-down version of the traditional Judeo-Christian idea of marriage. Some of them, reasonably enough on their premises, challenge the ideal of premarital chastity. Some others, however, cling to the ideal, somewhat irrationally. It seems very likely that most people uninfluenced by religious ideals and attitudes will find sexual intercourse between unmarried persons unobjectionable unless there is some element of exploitation or deceit or cruelty involved. On the other hand, if the Judeo-Christian view is correct, the prohibition of premarital intercourse is based on important facts about human nature and is given to us by the Creator of human nature. Can any light be cast on this question from a religiously neutral point of view?

One point which may be of importance is that those who defend premarital intercourse often seem to regard the sexual relationship between men and women as something relatively unimportant, as something which is "fun" or "friendly" or "warm," but nothing more. If making love is no more important than, for example, sharing a meal together, then these people's attitude is correct. But if sexual relationships between men and women are of major importance for their lives, their happiness, their development, then we may have to take a closer look at premarital sex.

The answer to the preliminary question seems obvious—sexual relationships affect our thoughts and attitudes in a major way, account for a great deal of happiness and unhappiness in our lives. Thus the question of how to live our sexual lives in such a way as to bring the greatest happiness to ourselves and others is of serious importance. Fortunately there is considerable human experience in the area of sexual relationships on which we can base some generalizations.

The human race has tried a number of social institutions in which to formalize sexual relationships. Polyandry, many husbands to one wife, has been rare, usually found only where women are few in proportion to men. Polygamy, many wives to one husband, has been frequent, but has almost always been accompanied by the idea that women were inferior beings—at worst, possessions; at best, childish and dependent. The form of marriage which usually accompanies a respect for women as persons is monogamy (or monandry)—one husband to one wife. Monogamous marriage, involving at least some degree of companionship or partnership, seems the most permanently satisfactory arrangement for satisfying emotional and sexual needs.

We can now ask whether premarital sexual relationships are likely to increase the chance of happiness in a monogamous relationship. There are two cases to consider: premarital relationships with persons other than the eventual spouse, or premarital relationships with the eventual spouse. Premarital relationships with others seem certain to cause strains in a monogamous marriage, but they may have advantages which outweigh this drawback. A good deal depends on whether the idea of "practicing" or "trying out" makes good sense with regard to a marriage relationship. (Steve, you will recall, suggested "seeing how we get along" to Laurie.)

The answer to this question depends a great deal on how marriage is regarded. If marriage is an unlimited commitment, then no limited commitment will really be a preparation for it, and this is true even of "trial marriages" with the eventual spouse. However, the relative ease of divorce in contemporary society makes the marriage commitment far from unlimited. "We can always divorce if it doesn't work out" and "We can live together and separate if it doesn't work out" are not greatly different in spirit.

So it becomes very much a matter of what attitudes and expectations we have concerning marriage. If we regard marriage as a serious commitment, normally lifelong, then experience suggests that premarital relationships are a poor preparation for happiness in such a relationship. If marriage is a very limited commitment, then the more limited commitment of simply living together is just a matter of degree. Whether any commitment should be total is a matter of our whole view of life. Some advocate a detached, cool attitude in human relationships, while others claim that only real commitments will bring lasting satisfaction. Thus sexual attitudes cannot be separated from our entire attitude toward life.

It may help to put sexual relationships in a wider context for, important as they are, they are only one kind of human relationship. Relationships between parents and children, between relatives, between friends, are also important.

One guide for personal relationships is a principle given by Immanuel Kant, the German philosopher. It is one formulation of the "Categorical Imperative," which Kant saw as the foundation of ethics. Kant's formulation was "so act as to treat other persons as ends, not merely as means." This can be explained in the following way: to treat other persons as a means is to disregard their wants, desires, ideas, opinions, and regard them merely as a way to obtain something which *we* want, perhaps sexual gratification, or money, or flattery, or some other advantage.

For the sultan, the members of his harem are precisely means to an end—his own gratification. Similarly the person who is promiscuous, heterosexually or homosexually, has no interest in those with whom he has sexual intercourse except as sex objects. The businessman who cultivates "friends" only for influence or financial return is similarly regarding them as means to his ends. "Mutual admiration societies" of "friends" who only flatter each other's egos are similarly using each other as means.

Of course to some extent we sometimes do have to regard people as means to our ends. A bus driver on a busy city route is for his passengers mainly a means to get them where they are going. The passengers cannot chat with him about the weather, inquire about his family, etc., without holding up his schedule or distracting his attention from driving. But suppose a driver has to leave his bus in mid-route because of illness or a family emergency. Do we think of him merely as a piece of machinery that has broken down, causing us inconvenience, or are we concerned for him as a fellow human being? If we think only of our own inconvenience, we are treating the driver *merely* as a means.

The same principle applies to more personal relationships. The teenager who regards her mother merely as a cook and laundress and chauffer; the father who tries to use his son merely to fulfill his own dreams of glory in high school or college athletics; the wife who treats her husband merely as a source of money and comfort, are all treating other human beings as means to their ends. Even if the person being exploited loves the exploiter enough that he or she doesn't resent the exploitation, the situation is not good for either party. To consent to be used *merely* as a means is to abdicate our humanity; to use others merely as means is to treat others inhumanly.

An idea similar to Kant's is expressed by the Jewish philosopher Martin Buber, who expressed it in terms of "I – it," "I – thou" relationships. "I – it" relationships are those it is appropriate to have to an *object*—a car, a piece of clothing, a meal, a chair. "I – thou" relationships are those it is appropriate to have to a person. What in Kant's terminology is treating a person merely as a means, Buber would call having an "I – it" relationship with him, treating him as an object. What Kant calls treating a person as an end in himself is in Buber's terminology having an "I – thou" relationship with him.

The weakness in both Kant's formulation and Buber's is that not all person-to-person relationships are morally desirable. Hate is an "I – thou" relationship as well as love. In hating someone we do not treat him as a means in any straightforward sense; we may be quite aware of his thoughts, feelings, wants, and desires, and use the awareness to cause him pain.

The Jewish and Christian principles, "Love your neighbor as yourself" and "Do to others as you would have them do to you" seem to include Kant's and Buber's insights while avoiding the difficulty just mentioned. To love someone is certainly to have an "I – thou" relationship with him; to treat others as you would want to be treated is certainly not to treat them merely as a means. But both these principles are easily misunderstood. Love as a feeling or emotion is not usually within our power to give or withhold. If loving your neighbor is interpreted as wanting what is good for him and trying to bring it about (as it is interpreted by Christ in the parable of the Good Samaritan), then it is something within our control. Furthermore, if loving our neighbor is interpreted as wanting the good of others and doing good to them when we can, it can be seen that "Love your neighbor" and "Do to others as you would have them do to you" are different ways of expressing the same point.

A possible confusion about "Do to others as you would have them do to you" is expressed by the quip, "No, don't do to others as you would have them do to you—their tastes may be different." But, of course, in applying the rule we must consider differences in taste and temperament. We might be grateful to have our faults pointed out bluntly—a touchier person might not. So in putting ourselves in their place we must take this into account: "If I were as insecure and easily upset as Sam, would I want my mistakes constantly called to my attention? Wouldn't I be more grateful if I were left to correct the mistakes myself and praised when I did a good job?"

Treating others as you would like to be treated *in their place* requires a certain amount of sensitivity and empathy, an ability to imagine how others are feeling or would feel. This, together with a willingness to act accordingly, is what we call "tact" or "considerateness" and it is undoubtedly a major factor in good personal relations. The ability to be tactful or considerate is not purely a matter of good will, it is partly a matter of experience and intelligence. Women often seem to be more tactful or considerate than men, probably for historical and cultural reasons. Social stereotypes portray women as being good at personal relationships, and men as being less easily offended and less tactful themselves. Since people often tend to live up to stereotypes, this is probably true to some extent.

Of course mere experience and intelligence without good will do not ensure consideration of others. The person who has a talent for personal relationships may use this talent to hurt or exploit. We prefer a tactless person who "means well" to a person who can put himself in our place but then uses this ability for his own ends. But tactlessness and lack of consideration based on ignorance or thoughtlessness may be culpable—loving your neighbor, or doing as you would be done to, requires us to apply intelligence to our personal relationships.

It may seem that I have been talking about good manners rather than about morals. But in personal relationships tact and consideration are of great practical and moral importance. Far from being mere "icing on the cake," they are quite essential. Family relationships, marriages, friendships can all be damaged or destroyed by lack of these qualities. "Good manners" in the sense of tact and consideration *is* good morals at a very practical level.

We tend to laugh nowadays at the customs of Victorian middle- and upper-class society, where children called their parents "Sir" and "Ma'am," and even husband and wife might address each other as "Mr. Smith" and "Mrs. Smith." But these customs did recognize that even in very personal relationships manners are necessary, and therefore tact and consideration are necessary.

Of course formal manners are not always expressions of tact and consideration. A person may use formal politeness to hurt others. Even people of good will may mistake formality for consideration. A friend of mine, in general a very considerate person, often addresses older men as "Sir." When old age was generally respected, this piece of formal good manners embodied genuine consideration for others. But nowadays when old age is often regarded with contempt rather than respect, many older people would prefer not to be reminded of their age by being treated differently from other people. I have observed that older men addressed by my friend as "Sir" do not always like it!

Perhaps we can now return to the subject of sexual ethics with a somewhat broader view. If concern for others' welfare—considerateness and tactfulness—is highly important in personal relations, it will be highly important in sexual relationships. A man who is genuinely concerned for a woman will take into account the fact that she may want marriage and a family, and that by having an affair with her without any intention of marriage he may be significantly decreasing her chances of marriage. A woman who enters into an affair with the idea of pressuring a man into marriage when in fact he doesn't really want to marry may be storing up unhappiness for both of them. Parents who object to premarital sex by their children may have to ask themselves whether they are concerned for their children's welfare, and if so on what grounds, or if they are concerned for their own social standing or social acceptance.

There might be those who disagree with what has just been said because they accept the Judeo-Christian view in its traditional form—lifelong commitment, total and exclusive, including prospective faithfulness to one's partner—as a guide to their own conduct. However, I do not see how we can reasonably apply this standard of conduct to those who do not accept the Judeo-Christian world-view and moral code. In some cases it might be argued that others *should* accept the Judeo-Christian view, that it would be unreasonable or unethical for them not to. But if they refuse, whether or not we can reasonably blame them for the refusal itself, we cannot reasonably blame them for not living up to a code which they do not accept. Similarly, we may blame someone for not taking on a job which he is perhaps uniquely qualified for. But whether or not we can reasonably blame him for his refusal, we cannot reasonably blame him for his failure to carry out the duties of the job he has refused.

This brings us to the question of "natural law." According to many religious views there is a "conscience" or "reason" or "law of our nature" given to man by God to guide his action. This law, put in an explicit form, is often called the "natural law." The question then arises whether natural law in this sense (the implicit moral judgments natural to human beings, organized and clarified into a code such as the Ross Rules) can be an adequate guide for action.

I would argue that no straightforward "yes" or "no" answer can be given. Certainly for a broad range of human action a code like the Ross Rules will give a workable guide to action. But there are cases, sexual ethics being one (suicide is another), where a religiously neutral code of ethics can give no final answers. A religious or anti-religious view or at least a world view of some kind must be added to purely ethical considerations. It might be the case that even if the universe is absurd and chaotic we should not harm others, should keep commitments, and so on. But anything we did with our own bodies insofar as it did not affect others, and anything we did with or to others with their consent, would seem to be ethically allowable.

Another way of putting the point is that in an absurd and purposeless universe the Ross Rule "Improve yourself" can only mean "Do what gives you maximum satisfaction (or avoids dissatisfaction)." Thus it would seem that suicide to avoid suffering would be morally unobjectionable, as would any kind of heterosexual or homosexual activity that was satisfactory to all parties concerned and did not harm anyone, break commitments, etc. On the other hand, if man is a creature of God and has a destiny beyond this life, then suicide might be an evasion of responsibility and some kinds of sexual activity might be inconsistent with God's plans or purposes.

It is worth noting on this point that the greatest pagan moralists (Socrates, Plato, and Aristotle, the Stoics, Confucius, and many others) diverge most widely from Christian ethical views in precisely the kinds of cases we have been discussing. This is inevitable, for such cases border on religion and ethics, and a difference of religious views will make a difference in ethical judgments.

One practical effect of this is in the relationship between law and morality. American society was originally pluralistic in the sense that its laws made no distinction between different forms of religious belief, but the laws did favor religious belief as against irreligion. Under the pressures of social change, the society has become pluralistic in a wider sense; the laws now make no distinction between religion and irreligion. This change can be seen, for example, in exemption from military service for conscientious objectors. Until a few years ago only religious grounds for conscientious objection to war were recognized. At present, objections based on a nonreligious world view are admitted, at least in theory, on an equal standing with objections on religious grounds.

As a consequence of this, society is now in the process of deciding whether such things as euthanasia with the consent of the person involved, homosexual "marriages" and the like, can reasonably be forbidden by law in a pluralistic society. It seems likely that many practices now forbidden by law will eventually be permitted on the grounds that society may not interfere with personal liberty unless there is general agreement that the acts forbidden are harmful to society. However, where the basis for holding certain acts as harmful is a religious or nonreligious world view, there will not be agreement as to whether they are harmful.

This does not mean that society must encourage any of these kinds of behavior—indeed, a pluralistic society cannot encourage any specifically religious or irreligious view *on the grounds that* it is religious or irreligious. A pluralistic society can, however, encourage or punish behavior on grounds of its utility for goals generally agreed on within that society. A *totally* pluralistic society, one in which *no* goals were agreed on, could not exist as a society, for a society can only exist where there is *some* agreement on goals (in practice, a great deal of agreement on goals is required for a workable society).

Since almost any society will agree on the undesirability of some forms of sexual behavior—rape, molestation of children—these can reasonably be forbidden, even in a pluralistic society. Forms of sexual behavior that are no longer regarded as morally wrong by many members of our society, such as extramarital heterosexual intercourse, are still forbidden by law in many states, but the laws are no longer enforced. Some forms of sexual behavior, such as homosexuality or group sex, are still regarded as morally wrong by the great majority of our society but are regarded as justifiable by vocal minorities. In such cases two principles of our society, majority rule and pluralistic neutrality, are in conflict. Where such issues are decided by popular vote, traditional prohibitions are maintained; where the issues are decided by courts of law, committed to pluralistic neutrality, such prohibitions are made void.

Supporters of traditional moral views are thus in a quandary; in the long run a pluralistic society cannot be expected to maintain the values they cherish, though for many reasons they may prefer a pluralistic society to one with an official religion. It would seem that the only solution for the supporter of traditional ethics in a pluralistic society is to try to convince others of the rightness of his view. Attempting to use the machinery of the State to enforce moral principles with which a large number of citizens sincerely disagree is, in the long run, not possible.

When early in this century the United States attempted to enforce prohibition of alcoholic beverages, otherwise law-abiding citizens ignored these laws, which they felt to be unjust and unreasonable. Nowadays, many young people, rightly or wrongly, have the same attitude toward laws prohibiting the use of marijuana. In both cases, Prohibition and current drug laws, enforcement was sporadic and generally ineffective, and probably more harm was done by lessening respect for law than was prevented by the prohibitory laws.

It does not necessarily follow that just laws should not be enforced even in the face of resistance and opposition. If this thesis were accepted, racial segregation would still be legal in many parts of the United States. But in areas of morality which affect mainly the individual's private life, legal intervention may do more harm than good.

DISCUSSION QUESTIONS

1. What advice would you give to Laurie? On what would you base this advice?
2. What kinds of sexual behavior are immoral? Why?
3. What kinds of sexual behavior are not immoral? Why?
4. What is your view of marriage? How does this view relate to your ethical views? Your religious views?
5. What institutions or practices in our society would change if people followed Kant's principle and never treated others *merely* as means?
6. What are the *practical* difficulties in doing to others as you would have them do to you?
7. How are manners related to morality?
8. What kinds of sexual behavior seem to treat other persons merely as means?
9. How do your religious views affect your views about sexual morality?
10. What kinds of personal behavior can a pluralistic society reasonably make laws about?

FURTHER READINGS

BEAUCHAMP, THOMAS, Ethics and Public Policy, Part 5. Englewood Cliffs, N.J.: Prentice-Hall, Inc., 1975:

DEVLIN, PATRICK, "Morals and the Criminal Law," pp. 241-251.

HART, H.L.A., "Social Solidarity and the Enforcement of Morals," pp. 252-264.

RACHELS, JAMES, *Moral Problems* (2nd ed.), Part 1. New York: Harper & Row, 1975:

NAGEL, THOMAS, "Sexual Perversion." pp. 3-15

RUDDICK, SARA, "On Sexal Morality." pp. 16-34

WASSERSTROM, RICHARD, *Today's Moral Problems,* Part 4. New York: The Macmillan Company, 1975:

BERTOCCI, PETER, "The Human Venture in Sex, Love and Marriage," pp. 218-232.

WASSERSTROM, RICHARD, "Is Adultery Immoral?" pp. 240-251.

Sexual and Racial Discrimination: Are Some More Equal Than Others? 8

Professor Pierce Sanders finally cornered his Department Chairman, Professor Williams, at the annual faculty party. "I've been looking for a talk with you for some time, James," he began.

"Well, Sandy, of course, anytime" replied Williams, "but you know, busy, busy, busy. In fact right now . . ."

"Right now we're going to have a little talk," said Sanders, pulling a straight chair over to the couch on which Williams was sitting. "It's about Joanna Edwards."

Williams smiled a trifle nervously. "She's a great asset to the department, Sandy, a great asset. Hiring a black woman put our affirmative action profile higher than any department in the college."

Sanders regarded his chairman dourly and a faint Scot's burr crept into his voice as he replied, "Maybe so, James man, maybe so, but she can't teach and she doesn't know anything about literature."

Williams looked uncomfortable as he said, "Well, now, Sandy, we mustn't be . . ."

He hesitated, and the other man looked at him quizzically as he replied: "Prejudiced? Bigoted? Aye, you're right and maybe I've done a bit more about prejudice than some other people on this faculty. But we mustn't condescend either, or let our guilt feelings about past mistakes push us to the opposite extreme."

Sanders pulled his chair closer and Williams, from the low couch, had to look up at him. "I'll tell you why I'm worried, James," continued the Scot. "I have a damned good student, Samantha Johnson, who's both black and a woman. She'd like to identify with Joanna, but she's too clever not to see that Joanna is several cuts below the other assistant professors. She told me the other day that she's not sure she wants to teach and find herself hired just to keep the federal money coming in. Luckily I think Fredricka Schiller can talk some sense into her."

Professor Williams looked a bit pettish. "Frankly, Sandy, I prefer Professor Edwards to Professor Schiller."

Sanders grinned. "I know you do, James. I'm not saying that Fredricka is an angel. I thought she'd cut my throat over that abortion debate. But Womens Lib or no, she earned her tenure and Associate Professorship by fine teaching and solid research. And if you wanted a black, why didn't you hire Dewey Johnson?"

Williams managed, with a wriggle and a twist, to get up out of the couch. "You know our tradition about not hiring our own graduates," he began.

Sanders sighed and got up from his chair also. "It's a tradition that's broken when we want to," he replied. "You're a case in point, aren't you, James? Well, if you won't discuss it, you won't; but I'll tell you two things. The first is that Fredricka and I are going to have to vote against tenure for Joanna. And the second is that I find your liberalism a little selective. I think you're really happier patronizing Joanna than you'd be with a competent young militant like Dewey. My standards are old-fashioned, I know. I'd prefer to consider only professional competence and forget race or sex. Maybe I'm wrong. Maybe women and blacks have some reparations due them and deserve special consideration. It's a hard problem, but I don't think that the solution is keeping on someone who can't cut the mustard because they're black and female and don't argue with the chairman." The Scot turned on his heel and strode off, his tall lanky frame and bony face looking curiously formidable as he pushed through the crowd.

The problem posed by our story is one which is peculiarly modern and peculiarly American. Minority groups, no longer content to demand equality, now demand reparation for past injustices. In the United States new laws enable the federal government to put heavy pressure on employers to hire minority members (this is called in government jargon the "affirmative action" program). Militant blacks, Indians, Chicanos, etc., picket and occupy buildings in pursuit of compensation for previous exploitation and prejudice. All of this raises complex moral problems.

A Ross Rule approach, and perhaps also a rule utilitarian approach, will grant the importance of making reparation for injuries done. But on the face of it, the obligation to make reparation seems to depend on your *own* evildoing. Can the *descendants* of an exploited group justly claim reparation from the *descendants* of the exploiter group? Even if so, how widely is "group" to be interpreted? If Professor Sanders' parents and grandparents were poor farmers in Scotland, and Joanna Edward's parents and grandparents were well-to-do middle-class blacks, does *he* owe *her* compensation? Can the entire "white race" (even if this concept were meaningful) be held responsible for slavery, exploitation, lynching, and so on? If not, what limits are to be set?

In addition, there are problems about equality. Is absolute equality an overriding value? Should everyone be treated just the same in every respect, regardless of age, sex, capacities, intelligence? If not, who should be treated differently, and why? In George Orwell's book *Animal Farm* the pigs cleverly used slogans of equality to secure their own ends. They started out with the slogan "All animals are equal," but as they began to claim privileges for themselves they added, "but some are more equal than others." When we treat minority groups with special consideration because of past injustices, are we making them "more equal" than others?

Let us begin with the idea of equality before the law, which is fairly clear-cut. When we say that all citizens are equal before the law, we mean that all *irrelevant* distinctions between them are to be ignored. It does not matter whether they are rich or poor, male or female, black, brown, yellow, red, or white—they are treated equally. But this does not mean that *relevant* differences are to be ignored. The guilty are treated differently from the innocent. Those who have shown themselves to be unreliable witnesses—for example, by past perjuries—are treated differently from reliable witnesses. Juvenile offenders are treated differently from adults.

When we move from the law courts to society in general, similar considerations would seem to apply. In applying for a job, ability to do the job is relevant, and other characteristics are relevant only insofar as they affect ability to do the job. Race is almost always irrelevant, so is sex, so is age. Consider a Shakespearean company: first they want competent Shakespearean actors, but a black actor might have some advantages for the role of Othello, a younger actress for Juliet, a male actor for Romeo, and so on.

Age might be relevant to occupations that require fine physical coordination, sex to occupations like locker-room attendant or lingerie salesperson. A Chinese restaurant might reasonably refuse to hire an Occidental chef, no matter how skilled, if they could reasonably expect that having a non-Chinese chef would lose them business.

As we can see by these examples, one way of stating a principle of fairness or equality is to "ignore irrelevant differences," or "treat relevantly similar cases similarly." This is almost a purely formal principle; it would seem to be irrational or unreasonable to treat relevantly similar cases differently. Ethical considerations would then enter in deciding which similarities were relevant.

However, in personal matters it becomes less clear that we must apply this kind of fairness principle, especially if "relevant difference" is to be defined in general ethical terms. As the proverb says, "Kissing goes by favor," and we choose our friends or lovers in ways that do not seem to fit into any general scheme. An enjoyment of Beethoven, or a taste for bad puns, or a vivacious disposition would be irrelevant to "public" cases such as courts of law or employment. But they may be very relevant to whom you make friends with or ask out on a date. Whether or not you enjoy the company of a person *is* a consideration that is relevant to whether you should accept an invitation from him or spend time with him. And factors like common tastes, or kinds of personality, are highly relevant to how comfortable we feel with people.

What about age, sex, race, etc., and personal relationships? Some people, it is true, find themselves comfortable only with people of their own sex (a "man's man," a "woman's woman"), or their own age or their own race. But those who are not blinded by prejudice or habit often find that the factors which make for friendship have no special relationship to race or age or sex. Erotic love is a more complex matter, of course; there are social and moral considerations involved. But very valuable and rewarding friendships can and do occur between men and women, between the old and the young, between people with very different racial or social backgrounds. However, fairness in this context does not assume equal treatment for all in the sense that everyone has an equal "right" to *be* your close friend. Rather, it assumes equal *opportunity;* no one is to be excluded *just* because of age, sex, race, etc.

This brings us to the question of equality of opportunity in the public sphere. If we are not determinists, we regard some things as being up to the individual, and we make a distinction between those who have an opportunity and make use of it, and those who, given the same opportunity, fail to use it through laziness or lack of interest. It seems "fair," in a somewhat different sense of fairness than we have been considering so far, that everyone should have an opportunity at some kinds of good things, and also "fair" or "just" that those who make use of the opportunity should have the good things and those who don't make use of it should not. This seems to be what we mean by "equality of opportunity."

There are several considerations here. First, equality of opportunity does not seem reasonable when applied to necessities of life. If there are thirty people, and food enough to feed twenty comfortably, the fair thing to do seems to be to divide the food equally so each person gets two-thirds of a normal portion, and no one goes hungry. It would not seem fair simply to let the thirty compete for the food so that twenty are well-fed and ten starve. But where necessities are not in question it does seem fair to reward more highly those who make a greater effort.

The difficulty with the last point is that greater effort is not always more effective than lesser effort, since success often depends on talents or abilities which are not evenly distributed. In some cases we handicap those with greater ability in order that effort should determine the outcome. In other cases this does not seem reasonable. Consider, for example, a school situation. The teacher may know that Mary, who is very bright, can do the ordinary schoolwork with little effort, whereas Johnny, who is hard-working but not as bright as Mary, must do a great deal more work to keep up. The teacher may reasonably give separate grades for effort and accomplishment, and it may be a good idea to give Mary more challenging work. But to ignore the difference between Mary's *accomplishments* and Johnny's is unfair to Mary, and may also be bad for Johnny in the long run. It may delude him as to his abilities, and when he faces a situation in which he is judged by accomplishment he may be in for a rude awakening.

One way in which one person can be at a disadvantage with respect to another is lack of training or education due to poverty or to racial or sexual prejudice. It is merely cynical to talk about equality of opportunity when those who already have the advantages are the only ones who can take advantage of the opportunities, so that the disadvantaged grow more disadvantaged.

That much is clear, but how to remedy the injustice is far less clear. Giving automatic preference to members of disadvantaged groups causes resentment among those in other groups whose opportunities are thus lessened. And unless the whole society can be controlled and a double standard always applied in every situation, sooner or later the system will break down. For example, in our story suppose that Professor Sanders is right about Professor Edwards. Sooner or later her students and colleagues will find themselves affected by her lack of knowledge of her subject matter and her inability to teach, and will have to come to a decision about how to shape their own behavior. Will students, given a choice, take her classes? Can her colleagues assign her courses that are important to the program of studies?

The other side of the coin is that if no attempt at compensation is made, "the rich get richer and the poor get poorer." Students from slum area schools will get worse educations and do less well on examinations for jobs or college entrance, whereas students from middle-class suburbs will do well on such tests. The children of the advantaged will become more advantaged, the children of the disadvantaged more disadvantaged. From a Ross Rule point of view it is important to note that duties of reparation take precedence over duties of simple fairness. The man from whom you have stolen money has greater claim to repayment than the man from whom you have borrowed money in the ordinary way. So for a Rossian or for a utilitarian who agrees that reparation takes precedence over simple fairness, the question of reparation becomes extremely important. Who may claim reparation? Who must make reparation?

Some cases are quite straightforward. If the telephone company has for many years discriminated against female employees, as was claimed in a court case some time ago, then that company, a continuing corporate entity, owes compensation to those individuals formerly employed or still employed who were injured. (This is just what the court decided in that case.) But consider, for example, a law school faced with demands for "reparations" by women and racial minority groups. The school may claim, with some degree of truth, that there was never an official policy excluding women or racial minorities, but that for a variety of reasons almost none applied. Furthermore, it is quite difficult to identify a recognizable group as having been harmed. All women and all racial minorities? Just those who might have applied but didn't? One group seems too large, the other too small.

The group actually making the claim to preferential admission often has no direct connection with persons who may have previously been denied admittance. What they might reasonably claim is that as women or members of racial minorities, they are members of the class "women or members of racial minorities seeking admission to law school." If *this* group has been unfairly discriminated against in the past, then members of *this* group can claim compensating preferential treatment now. In a similar way, a university, a church, a company, may be regarded as continuing entities which may owe obligations of reparation to specified groups. This may be hard on those who are presently the representatives or officers of those institutions, but since these persons inherit many benefits from their predecessors, it is only fair that they inherit some liabilities.

Thus, Professor Sanders may well owe to his predecessors at the university a great many things—the buildings he teaches in, the reputation of his department, the tradition of his subject. If some of these benefits come to him from predecessors who treated women or minorities unfairly, Sanders may be thought to owe some reparation to the "successors" (in a broad sense) of those discriminated against.

Note that the claim being made is not for charity or beneficence; rather, it is a claim about what is due in justice to the members of previously disadvantaged groups. This is important because while fairness takes precedence over beneficence, reparation takes precedence over simple fairness, according to the Ross Rules. Another important point is that the obligation holds between groups of people which are in some sense continuing groups, in which both benefits and obligations can be inherited. Merely as an individual, Professor Sanders may have no special obligations to Professor Edwards, and it would seem that he has no obligations to her as a member of the group "Scots Highlanders," or the group "pipe smokers." But as a member of the group "professor at a university which has discriminated against blacks and women," he may have a responsibility.

Supposing that someone does have an obligation to make reparation, what does this obligation involve? To answer this question it will be useful to take a look at the main kinds of harm people can do to each other and the kinds of reparation that are possible in each case.

The first general category of harm seems to be physical harm. Some kinds of physical harm, like murder, maiming, or mutilation, are permanent and it does not seem that any adequate reparation can be made for them. On the other hand, temporary physical harm, such as wounding, or damage to health, or causing of physical pain, can to some extent be reversed; the person can be healed, cured, or comforted. Imprisonment or confinement is a kind of physical harm in a wider sense, and in such cases the prisoner can be freed and perhaps compensated in some way. Loss of property or its use, which is physical harm in a very extended sense, can most easily be remedied; stolen property can be restored or replaced.

Since money is our general medium of exchange, we usually consider that monetary compensation is at least partial reparation for physical harm. A family may be compensated partially for the loss of a breadwinner (perhaps in a fatal automobile crash) by payments which take the place of the wages the person might have earned. Loss of limbs or mutilation is also partially compensated by monetary payments, as are things like wounding, causing pain, or unlawful confinement or false imprisonment. It is not that we consider that money can ever be full compensation in such cases, but that a monetary payment is often the best we can do at reparation. Where medically possible we might approve of reparations "in kind," for example, the donation of a kidney or an eye to replace one damaged by our fault, presuming that there were no legal or moral barriers. In cases of loss of property, on the other hand, monetary payment is often considered to be full compensation, and in some cases we are even pleased at a loss if we are well compensated for it (e.g., "That stereo was never any good; I'm just as happy to have the insurance money").

Kinds of harm other than physical pose a more complex problem. Suppose that an action of ours drives someone insane, or inflicts great mental anguish on someone. Aside from attempting to cure or comfort them we might try to improve their mental stability or to give them greater happiness. Where our actions have inflicted fear or anxiety on others, we can attempt to free them from these fears and to make them more serene or secure if this is within our power. The type of mental harm that is easiest to deal with is having deceived someone or kept him in ignorance; in such cases we can undeceive or enlighten him. Presumably one justification for programs of ethnic studies, women's studies, etc., in schools is that these programs make some reparation for past lies or suppression of facts about these groups.

It can be noticed that mental harm is not so easy to inflict against the resistance of the victim as physical harm. The last category of harm, moral harm, seems always to involve some cooperation by the victim. We cannot morally corrupt or deprave someone without his consent, and even if our injuries or insults give him reason to hate us, it is up to him whether or not he gives way to hatred or anger or resentment. Similarly, we cannot make someone overscrupulous or cause false guilt in him without some cooperation on his part, and the same goes for preventing a person from acquiring virtues or good habits.

In all of these cases the only possible reparation seems to be to help the person, insofar as possible, to achieve the moral good he has lost—helping him acquire good habits or a sound conscience, helping him to forgive, helping him to become morally better. Monetary compensation would seem grotesque if offered in reparation for a moral injury, and any merely intellectual good would hardly seem adequate compensation. Of course, in all cases of reparation it seems obligatory to do whatever is in our power to make up for an injury to others, even if this is very inadequate. But the best reparation would seem to be something as nearly as possible opposite to the injury done. Bringing the victim to life again, if it were only possible, would seem the best reparation for murder, for instance.

Certainly, past injuries such as enslavement, discrimination, or exploitation can do moral harm by causing hatred and bitterness in the victims. But although religious institutions may be able to repair some of these moral harms by preaching, teaching, and counseling, governmental or corporate or educational institutions can do little in this area, and would be well advised not to try. But while there seems nothing that governmental or corporate bodies can do to bring about moral goods as reparation for moral injuries, they can certainly try to repair past intellectual harm by education, by setting the record straight on past lies or propaganda, and so on.

It is worth noting that when we harm others by way of legal punishment it is always physical harm that is used, and usually those kinds of physical harm, such as deprivation of property (fines or forfeitures) or imprisonment, which can be measured out in degrees. Sometimes in personal relationships we try to "get back" at others by causing them worry, guilt, fear, and so on, but there seems to be serious doubt as to whether such "punishments" can be justified. The State, at any rate, has no business trying to inflict such punishments; nor, of course, could it ever be justifiable for anyone to try to inflict moral harm as a punishment.

Let us now return to cases where women or ethnic minority members are claiming reparation for past discrimination. Presumably one major complaint is against past deprivation of *opportunities,* and a reasonable reparation is to give *extra* opportunities, more opportunities than would be available under the rule of simple fairness. To speak quasi-mathematically, if over a period of a hundred years some minority should, on the basis of simple fairness, have had five of the openings at a given law school per year, then it is not enough to simply begin to give them that number of places from now on. There is a "backlog" of 500 places previously denied. In practical terms this might have to be spread out over a number of years, but if that number of places are due in reparation, then there is an obligation to make them available.

But suppose over the period of time decided on there are not 500 qualified minority members who wish to take advantage of the opportunity. Surely, it may be argued, it is only *qualified* members of the minority group who can claim sufficient identity with those discriminated against in the past. Thus if only 50 qualified applicants appear for the 500 places, it may seem that the law school is able to satisfy its obligation to make reparation rather cheaply.

It is precisely here that some of the most difficult questions arise. Is the law school obliged to accept *and graduate* applicants who are not at all qualified to study law? Surely not. Is the school satisfying its obligations by accepting and flunking out unqualified persons? Obviously not. What then is the school to do?

Some obvious practical solutions are for the school to make special efforts to seek out well-qualified minority applicants and to give marginally qualified minority applicants special help to successfully complete their studies. But there is a point beyond which such efforts are self-defeating. If the school allows minority members lower standards for graduation, then it devalues the degrees of *all* minority members, no matter how able. At some stage graduates will have to deal with some group who will feel no obligation to give them favored status—those who grade the bar examination, or at least those who are prospective clients.

Thus there is a limit to favored treatment as compensation for past injuries, and minority members, even if given special opportunities, may have to work much harder for the same success that comes easily to those more advantaged by ancestry or background. But in general, reparation can never entirely make up for an injury, and a sincere effort to make as much reparation as possible is all that morality can demand.

The question of "quota systems" in jobs or other opportunities raises questions of equality as well as questions of reparation. For example, granted that women are 50 percent of the population, should 50 percent of doctors, astronauts, professional athletes, college students, and the like be women? There seem to be two considerations which are especially relevant here: interest and ability. If you are the admissions officer at Western University and have 1,000 places for freshmen, should you choose the 1,000 best applicants regardless of sex, or should you choose the best 500 female applicants and the best 500 male applicants? If you are the athletic director at Western University, should you allot 50 percent of your budget to men's athletics and 50 percent to women's athletics, or should you allot more money to the programs that arouse more interest? Should 50 percent of the places at Western Medical School be reserved for women and 50 percent of the places at its School of Nursing be kept for men, without regard to the number of applicants likely to be interested?

There are, of course, some people who would answer "yes" to all of these questions. In some cases the reasons might be pragmatic; many more women doctors and many more male nurses are needed, and a "50 percent policy" might encourage more of each. Again, women's sports have often been underfunded and deserve greater support. But aside from reasons obtaining in special cases, the idea that each human activity should be divided up by sexual and racial quotas seems absurd. Equality in the sense of equality before the law or equality of opportunity will regard sex and race as irrelevant factors in most cases. Reparations for past injustices may lead to increased opportunities for those previously discriminated against, but this will not lead to a quota system in the sense we have been discussing. In fact, it is hard to see what justifiable moral principle could lead to a quota system.

With regard to reparation for past discrimination in job situations, there are a number of complicating factors. Granted that increased job *opportunities* are offered in partial compensation for past discrimination, should favored treatment be continued *on* the job? Besides the rights of members of groups previously discriminated against, we have to consider the rights of their fellow workers and of those who are affected by how well the job is done.

Almost anyone would agree that outright incompetence should not be ignored or protected. But suppose that because of past discrimination members of some minority group are generally less efficient at some job than nonminority members. The lesser efficiency is not their fault, and if efficiency is the only criterion, the already favored majority group will continue to have the advantage, an advantage based on past injustices. On the other hand, favored treatment because of minority status will cause resentment among fellow workers and may harm the interests of those who depend on the job's being done well. Furthermore, favored treatment based on race or sex may damage the self-respect of those being favored. They may feel that their talents or accomplishments or hard work are not the real cause of their success; they may find being patronized as objectionable as being discriminated against. Most of us want to feel that our success is due to ourselves, not our race or sex.

There are no easy answers to this problem. At best we can choose a solution which seems to offer the best chance of remedying past injustices without causing new ones. In practice the following points seem to be the elements of such a solution:

1. Considerable time, money, and effort should be expended on recruiting members of previously disadvantaged groups.
2. When recruited, they should be offered special training or help to overcome disadvantages arising from previous discrimination.
3. Probationary periods might reasonably be extended for them in order to allow them maximum opportunities to adapt to new situations.
4. Policies which tend to put at a disadvantage those previously discriminated against (involving such things as family situation, language, place or hours of work, etc.) should be carefully reviewed to see how essential they are to the purpose of the job.
5. At some stage special or favored treatment should cease and from that stage on all workers should be judged solely on their individual talents and effort.

The last point is especially important for the self-respect of the minority group involved and the respect with which they are regarded by their fellow workers. A compensatory "head start" will cause resentment among some, but most people will see the justice of it where there has been previous discrimination. But continued favoritism will in the long run damage the minority group more than it helps them. Reparation is an attempt to restore the balance of justice. But since injustice on one side is not compensated for by injustice on the other side, we must be sure that our attempts to restore the balance do not lead to new injustices.

DISCUSSION QUESTIONS

1. Suppose that Professor Sanders is right about the facts in the case of Professor Edwards. Do you agree or disagree with his attitude? Why or why not?
2. In the slogan "Equal rights for women," what kinds of equality seem to be being demanded?
3. Is the question of equality for women different from the question of equality for ethnic minorities? If so, in what way?
4. What special problems would there be in a demand for "Equal rights for children"?
5. Would a demand for "Equal rights for animals" be absurd? Why or why not?
6. Would the considerations in this chapter apply to demands for equal rights for homosexuals? Why or why not?
7. To what extent do you agree or disagree with the discussion in this chapter on reparation to groups previously discriminated against? Give your reasons for agreeing or disagreeing.
8. Discuss the special problems of making reparation in some specific case (e.g., Jews in Germany, blacks in the United States, women in some organized church).
9. What improvements could you make in the suggested solution to the problem of reparations in job situations?
10. What points in this chapter did you agree with or disagree with most strongly? Why?

FURTHER READINGS

Beauchamp, Thomas, *Ethics and Public Policy*, Part 1. Englewood Cliffs, N.J.: Prentice-Hall, Inc., 1975:

Hughes, Graham, "Reparations for Blacks?" pp. 20-30.

Nagel, Thomas, "Equal Treatment and Compensatory Discrimination," pp. 44-55.

Rachels, James, *Moral Problems* (2nd ed.), Part 3. New York: Harper & Row, 1975:

LUCAS, J. R., "Because You Are a Woman." pp. 132-143.

THOMSON, JUDITH JARVIS, "Preferential Hiring." pp. 144-162

WASSERSTROM, RICHARD, *Todays Moral Problems,* Part 3. New York: The Macmillan Company, 1975:

BOXILL, BERNARD R., "The Morality of Reparation," pp. 209-215.

NEWTON, LISA H., "Reverse Discrimination as Unjustified," pp. 204-208.

9 Ecology and Ethics: Do Trees Have Rights?

Jean Kane pressed her fingertips against her closed eyelids. She was beginning to feel a headache coming on. Mr. McWhortle, next to her, was still booming on; like Fred Kresnick before him, he was going to take more than his share of the time. Jean made herself pay attention to what he was saying. She knew most of it by heart from previous meetings of a similar kind. Locked-up natural resources, the need for timber, the need for jobs, the need for a tax base. As a schoolteacher Jean could appreciate the need for taxes, but she had a shrewd idea that it was the ramifications of his own business interests that brought Joe McWhortle here to oppose the extension of the National Park. McWhortle had shrewdly turned the self-interest issue against Kresnick, not too subtly reminding the audience that Fred was a paid lobbyist for a coalition of conservation groups.

Jean didn't think that that shot had impressed the audience; Kresnick, in his shabby suit, was obviously making no fortune fighting for the ecology. But Fred hadn't really gripped the audience either; his enthusiasms were too different from theirs. McWhortle was building on that now, using his bluff just-an-ordinary-fellow manner: "Now, Mr. Kresnick has told us, folks, that he considers that us humans have no right to disturb the environment."

Kresnick looked up suddenly, his bushy hair and beaky nose somehow giving him the appearance of Woodstock in the *Peanuts* comic strip. "I said *destroy*," he snapped out in his New England twang.

McWhortle smiled, his chubby visage looking misleadingly benevolent. "Well, now, if we hadn't destroyed some of the environment I guess this town or this building wouldn't be here now," he retorted. "I guess if it comes to saving a tree or feeding a hungry child, I'll feed the child every time. Mr. Kresnick seems to talk as if trees have rights just like people. I guess that's the difference between us: he's in favor of the rights of trees, I'm in favor of the rights of people!" Obviously pleased with his own rhetoric, he hesitated a moment, then sat down as if deciding he couldn't do better than that to cap his speech.

Jean Kane had a moment of panic, but classroom reflexes pulled her through. She rose without haste, and waiting till she had their attention, began drily, "I don't know about the rights of trees. . . ." Some sympathetic grins in the audience heartened her, and she went on: ". . . but I do know a little about the rights of people, especially the rights of children. I want our children and our grandchildren and our great-grandchildren to be able to enjoy the trees and the mountains and the streams and the animals, as we did when we were young. I don't want all the trees cut down just because Joe McWhortle wants to sell chainsaws, or all the deer shot to fill freezers with venison people don't eat and can't give away."

Jean felt a slight pang at slipping in that reference to McWhortle's business interest in the proposed logging, but he'd asked for it with his remarks about Kresnick. She went on: "I like living here in the Valley; I like the unspoiled views and the clean air and pure water. I'm proud to show off the Park to friends and relatives, and although I don't think much of some of the tourists that come, maybe if we lived all crowded together as some of them do, we'd be a little more short-tempered and impatient too. I'm glad we have the Park for them and for us and for all our children and children's children. Not all of us can backpack through the high country like Mr. Kresnick, but all of us can enjoy the Park in some way. If the proposed extensions are approved maybe all of us, including the school board, will be a little poorer in terms of money than if that timber were cut and sold. But I think we'll be richer in other ways. I don't know if I can buy all of what Mr. Kresnick said about the unity of life and the Indians' religion of nature—I'm a Methodist myself. But I do feel a sense of stewardship. We're responsible for this country, responsible to our countrymen and responsible to future generations. I'd like to see the vote of the County Commissioners reflect that responsibility." She sat down, feeling a little foolish, but also a little proud, with her neighbors' applause in her ears.

This story raises the issue of ethics as applied to ecological issues, but it also raises the issue of rights. Must we consider the rights of future generations as well as the rights of those living now? What sort of right is the right to pure air and water? Is there a "right to wilderness"? Can we legitimately talk of the rights of animals or the right of an ancient forest to continue to exist? To answer such questions, we must answer old problems about the nature of human rights and about the relation of man to nature, as well as new questions about pollution and ecology.

Let us begin with rights. Rights and obligations are closely related. If I have a right, then usually someone has an obligation to uphold that right. If the right is a legal one, then courts and law enforcement officials are legally obligated to uphold it. If the right is a moral right without legal backing—for example, a right based on a private promise—then some individual or individuals are morally obligated. Some rights are both legal and moral, some only moral. There may be some legal rights which are not moral rights, as we will see in due course.

It would seem that rights and duties hold only between persons. I cannot have a duty to a chair and a chair can have no rights. To say that I "have a right to" a chair means in fact that I have a right to use that chair, and other persons have a duty not to prevent me. I may have duties which *concern* a chair, but these are duties to persons; for example, a duty to deliver a chair undamaged to a certain person. But all rights and all duties seem to be, in the last analysis, relations between two or more persons.

Can we have duties towards persons who are not yet born? It would seem clear that we can. Suppose, for example, that I set a booby trap which is sure to be discovered a hundred years from now, and which will explode, killing whoever opens it. Surely to set such a booby trap is morally wrong, even though the person who would be injured is not yet born. Similarly, if I pollute the land, water, or air in a way which will adversely affect future generations, what I do is morally wrong, even if no one *now* living is adversely affected. Thus we can say that I have obligations not to harm people yet unborn, and conversely, that they have a right not to be harmed by me.

This kind of argument, that pollution, destruction of wilderness, extinction of animal species, etc., harm future generations, is one often used by ecologists and it perhaps is the most straightforward argument in this area. Private profit does not justify harming people, whether those are people now living or people yet to be born.

But suppose, for the sake of argument, that some kind of environmental destruction does not adversely affect other human beings, either those now living or those yet to be born. What moral considerations would apply in that case? For the religious believer there is a clear and obvious answer. For the traditional theist the natural world is the creation of God, and man is responsible to God for his use of that creation. The religious believer who feels that nature as a whole, or particular aspects of nature, in some way embodies a personal or quasi-personal spirit or spirits will also be able to see the sense in rights and obligations with regard to the natural world. On the other hand, a materialist would seem to have no grounds for a theory of ecological rights or obligations unless the interests of other human persons were involved.

It would seem, then, that there are two classes of "ecological obligations." The first, less controversial class consists of obligations not to harm other human persons, including those yet unborn, by damaging the environment. The second, more controversial class consists of obligations not to harm animals or plant life, damage natural environment, etc., where no harm to other human beings results.

The first class of ecological obligations is simply a special case of the Ross Rule obligation not to do things which are likely to harm others. Polluting or damaging the environment can cause death or illness to others, damage their property, or spoil their enjoyment of it. Either the Rossian or the utilitarian will condemn such behavior.

But the second class of ecological obligations is less straightforward. Let's forget animals for the moment, since they seem at least quasi-personal. Suppose that I own a small valley in the mountains of California, remote and inaccessible, which contains a magnificent grove of ancient first-growth redwood trees. Suppose, for the sake of argument, that it is very unlikely that anyone else will visit the valley or enjoy the trees. Would I be justified in setting the trees on fire and devastating the valley merely to enjoy a spectacular forest fire?

If only humans have rights, and if I am the only human involved, then the answer would seem to be "yes." If, on the other hand, we are only the stewards of Creation, such an act of wanton destruction would be wrong, even though it harms no human. However, it might not be wrong to cut down those trees if they were the only source of material to build houses for homeless people. On the traditional theistic view, man must respect nature, but has a right to use it for his needs. Some religious or quasi-religious views, however, would deny man even this right, on the grounds that all forms of life are in some sense equal, but only a small group would hold such a view and it is hard to see how they could convince others to share it.

Let us try, then, to set down a sort of ecological code of ethics which might recommend itself to reasonable persons, starting with the more obvious principles, and going on to more disputed ones:

1. No one shall affect the environment[1] in such a way as to harm other persons, either living or still to be born, except to prevent greater harm to present or future persons.
2. The environment may be used for human needs, where this does not conflict with Rule 1.
3. The environment is to be preserved and protected, where this does not conflict with Rules 1 and 2.

Stated in the broad and general form, the rules may seem relatively uncontroversial. Rule 1 would forbid many of the usual kinds of pollution; rule 2 would allow the use of plants and animals for food, shelter, etc.; and rule 3 would protect the environment against wanton destruction. But of course, as with most general rules, the controversy comes in applying the rules to disputed cases. Food, shelter, and colthing are human necessities, but what about foods which can be obtained only by cruel treatment of animals, building or heating materials whose procurement devastates scenic beauty, and clothing, such as furs, which endangers animal species? Even within guidelines, such as the relatively moderate rules listed above, there is plenty of room for debate about whether our life style is damaging to the environment.

Two factors complicate the issue. First, men desire not only to survive but also to live well. A house of cinderblock may be adequate shelter, but a house of redwood is more satisfying. Meat is tastier than soybeans; and many uses of electrical power, such as television or Christmas lighting, are not necessary for survival but add greatly to our enjoyment of life. To what extent, then, should we give up our luxuries and amenities to save the environment?

The second complicating factor is population. The primitive peoples

[1] I use this term in the familiar modern sense to include animals, plants, scenery, etc.

who live in harmony with their environment make fewer demands on it than civilized man, but they are also very few in number. As population increases, pressure on the environment increases, even if the standard of living is far from luxurious, as can be seen in countries like India. The eventual solution might be a greatly decreased population, but there are two difficulties with this. One is practical: given the present population of the world, a drastic decrease in population will take a long time. The other problem is theoretical: if life is a good thing, should not as many people as possible enjoy it? On these grounds it would seem a good thing to *increase* the population rather than decrease it. Of course, at some stage quality of life would become intolerably low, but crowded countries, like Japan, demonstrate that population density can be very high and quality of life can still be maintained.

There are thus a great number of questions to be answered before we can give a reasonable solution to problems of ecological ethics. In fact, like many questions in ethics, the ultimate answers lie only in our total view of life. What is human life all about? What is man's relation to the universe? Until we answer those questions we cannot really balance the questions of quality of life versus number of lives, human necessities versus damage to the environment. If the universe is meaningless and doomed to eventual destruction, a little more destruction of the environment doesn't seem to matter a great deal. On the other hand, if man is accountable to God for the use of all the gifts which have been given to him, misuse of the environment may be a failure in this responsibility. A belief that man is part of nature, and that all life and all beauty must be treated with reverence, would also lead to respect for the environment; but this belief, though strongly felt by some, is not widely shared and seems hard to communicate to those who do not share it.

In this case, then, as in the cases of sexual ethics and of suicide, religious beliefs in a wide sense will affect our ethical judgments. It may be wise, therefore, to take another look at the relation of ethics to religious belief. A good starting point would be the question of rights. In the traditional view, as expressed, for example, in the Declaration of Independence, rights are God-given: "All men are created equal, endowed by their Creator with certain inalienable rights, . . . among these are Life, Liberty, and the Pursuit of Happiness." On this traditional view each human being, simply because he or she is human, has these rights, and these rights are "inalienable": they cannot be taken away.

At the other extreme is the view that there are no "natural rights"; that the only rights anyone has are legal rights. According to this view, in the absence of laws no one has rights, and whatever rights any person has are just those which they are allowed by the law. In between these two extremes—the God-given rights view and the purely legalistic view of rights—are other possible views, for example the view of some humanists that persons have natural rights which are more than just legal rights, but which are not given to man by God.

One such intermediate view is the "contract" view of human rights, which says that by living together in society we make an implicit agreement to recognize certain rights and obligations. An ingenious modern version [2] of such a "contract" theory starts off with a commonplace example of fair play. Suppose a mother is too busy to divide a cake evenly between two children. She might say, "Mark, you cut the cake and Tim is to have first choice." Knowing that Tim will choose the bigger piece (and he will be left with the smaller) if he cuts unequally, Mark will take great care to make an equal division.

Generalizing the principle involved, we can say that a fair allocation of anything, including rights and responsibilities, would be one which we would make if we knew we would have the last choice.[3] If we had to make an allocation of rights and obligations on that basis we would take care to see that the allocation was as equitable as possible since, if there was a share markedly worse than the others, we would probably be left with it. The ingenuity of the theory lies in the fact that we have gotten a principle of fairness out of considerations which are basically self-interested.

A principle of fairness based on this kind of theory would seem to justify universal human rights, at least of the more obvious kind. Since no one would himself want to be deprived of life or liberty or the opportunity to seek happiness, it would seem unfair for anyone to deprive others of these rights. Some more subtle rights, such as freedom of religion, freedom of artistic expression, and so on, seem less susceptible to this treatment, since a person with no religious beliefs or with no artistic inclinations might be undisturbed at a division of rights and obligations which left out such freedoms. Similar considerations apply to environmental rights and obligations. Someone indifferent to the beauty of nature would be undisturbed by an allocation of social rights and responsibilities which ignored environmental rights and obligations.

Furthermore, there are serious difficulties in the contract theory itself, even in the ingenious variation we have just described. For, although the thought experiment of asking what allocation of rights and responsibilities we would make if we had last choice is a useful way of *defining* or *under-*

[2] See John Rawls, *A Theory of Justice* (Cambridge: Harvard University Press, 1974) for the most sophisticated modern development of such a theory.

[3] The principle is sometimes stated as a division we would make if we didn't know which part we would get but this is less satisfactory; a gambler might make an unequal allocation, hoping to be lucky.

standing fairness, it does not give us a motive or reason for *acting* in a fair or just way. The egoist can perfectly well point out that he is *not* in the position of having the last choice, and what he would do if he *were* in that position does not by itself determine what he should do in the real situation.

Of course a recognized principle of fairness can be imposed by society by the use of punishments and rewards, but this brings us back to the view that the only rights and obligations are legal rights and obligations. It might seem that the theory that rights are God-given merely bases rights on rewards and punishments by God to back up rights, rather than basing them on rewards or punishments by society. But, as we noted earlier, the most plausible religious theory of ethics bases morality on the nature of man and the nature of God, rather than merely on commands of God backed by rewards and punishments.

The person who rejects religious belief will, of course, reject any religious justification for human rights. He will have to base human rights on something other than a divine plan or purpose. His appeal must be to something else, perhaps to human nature, or to the consensus of informed and concerned persons.

But what can this appeal be? Consider environmental rights—there is far from being a general consensus on such rights. Many human beings are far too worried about their own survival to worry about the environment. Others put some other value (success, knowledge, power) much higher than environmental values. If human nature is merely the accidental result of forces without plan or purpose, it is hard to see what rights can be based on human nature. And if it is merely a matter of choice or affirmation, how can one person's affirmation convince another person?

It is not surprising, then, that many defenders of environmental values appeal, explicitly or implicitly, to a religious or quasi-religious view of the universe. Some such appeals are to traditional theism, others to a view which ascribes some sort of divinity to nature as a whole or life as a whole. The justification of environmental rights would then depend on the justification of the religious view involved, but a nonreligious justification of environmental rights seems unlikely.

A question that is often raised about environmental rights is their relative importance in a world where there is so much human suffering and need. Suppose that I receive an appeal from the Save the Redwoods Federation, and also an appeal from CARE for starving victims of a natural disaster. It might be agreed that the starving people are more important than the endangered redwoods, and that if I can contribute to only one organization it ought to be one like CARE. But even supposing that I *can* contribute to both, *should* I? Shouldn't I forget the redwoods and contribute all the money I can spare to the starving people?

In practice, I myself do not follow this course. I contribute most to organizations which help relieve suffering and meet human needs, but I make some contributions to organizations which protect or improve the environment. I would justify this mainly in terms of human needs. "Man does not live by bread alone"; we need beauty and peace as well as food and shelter. But I can understand and have considerable sympathy with those who feel that human needs should take precedence over environmental considerations, so long as this is not merely an excuse. Some of those who oppose environmental considerations are merely using this stand to further their own ends, like McWhortle in our story. Others refuse to concern themselves with environmental problems because human problems are more important, and then do nothing about the human problems.

Environmental rights have only recently been recognized as an ethical issue, and the reason for this is fairly obvious. Questions of value are often brought to our attention by scarcity. So long as there was plenty of unspoiled country, abundant pure air and water, the spoiling of some areas seemed unimportant. But the increasing scarcity of pure air and water, and of country unspoiled by "civilization," emphasizes the value of these things. Now that the questions of environmental ethics have been brought to our attention, we must begin to do some serious thinking about these questions.

DISCUSSION QUESTIONS

1. Look at some literature put out by an environmental group such as the Sierra Club or Friends of the Earth. What claims are made? Which of these are ethical claims? What ethical or religious (in a wide sense) assumptions are being made?
2. Do the same with some statement by a group or individual opposed to the goals of environmental groups.
3. What are some ways in which we can harm others by misusing the environment? What ethical issues does each involve?
4. What human needs (if any) should take precedence over environmental considerations?
5. What human needs or desires (if any) should take second place to environmental considerations?
6. How (if at all) can the environment be harmed without harming human beings?
7. What rules (if any) would you add to the suggested code of environmental ethics? What rule (if any) would you remove or modify? Why?

8. How do your religious beliefs (or lack of religious beliefs) affect your attitude towards environmental ethics?

9. On what basis would you divide time or money between human needs and environmental causes?

10. How might McWhortle reply to Jean Kane's speech? How does her position fit the code of environmental ethics proposed in this chapter?

FURTHER READINGS

BEAUCHAMP, THOMAS, *Ethics and Public Policy*, Part 7. Englewood Cliffs, N.J.: Prentice-Hall, Inc., 1975:

GOLDING, MARTIN P., "Ethical Issues in Biological Engineering," pp. 393-408.

KASS, LEON R., "The New Biology: What Price Relieving Man's Estate?" pp. 370-392.

RACHELS, JAMES, *Moral Problems* (2nd ed.), Part 3. New York: Harper & Row, 1975:

SINGER, PETER, "Animal Liberation." pp. 163-177.

10 Ethical Motivation: How Should We Behave?

Midge Kelly always felt vaguely dissatisfied after her talks with Professor Bowman. If someone had told her that this was because he treated her as he treated any other student she would have denied it indignantly, but there was no denying that most people did treat her differently. Her raven black hair and dark blue eyes, added to a beautiful face and figure, would have been enough to gain her special attention, but added to this her petite size and a rather wistful quality in her gaze made most older men feel protective and paternal, or at least avuncular. But Professor Bowman's bland face showed no softening as he looked at Midge, and despite his general air of vagueness and untidiness, he never missed a point in an argument. He pounced immediately on any weakness or unclarity in a position, and Midge never felt she'd won an argument with him, or even that she'd done justice to her own opinions.

At the moment, she was having to back down—a process she disliked intensely. "All right, Professor Bowman, I'll admit that I was wrong about the ethical principles we've been talking about in class having no relation to our everyday lives. In fact, I've even been driving more carefully since we discussed in class how the ordinary person's greatest likelihood of really hurting other people physically was by causing an automobile accident. And there's things I've been noticing more about keeping commitments I've made and helping other people, and like that. But I don't see how any of what we've talked about can make a person want to do right if they don't want to."

Midge paused, feeling that hadn't come out quite right, and then plunged ahead. "I mean, if a person doesn't *care* whether they hurt a person, what use is studying Ethics then? How can you convince a person how they should behave just by studying Ethics?"

Professor Bowman finished filling his pipe and brushed some fallen tobacco from his well-rounded stomach, missing several crumbs that had found their way into the wrinkles of his vest. "If you merely mean," he began, "that there is a difference between knowing and wanting, well of course there is. I know perfectly well that tobacco is bad for me but I have the desire to puff away anyhow. You can see a reason without acting on it. But if you mean that moral philosophy can't give good reasons for behaving morally, then you're wrong. If a man is open to reason, Ethics can give him reasons for moral behavior."

"What kind of reasons?" Midge challenged.

Bowman raised a bushy eyebrow. "It seems to me that we've talked about some of them in class. In a way each of the theories we've talked about point out one direction we can look for a reason to behave morally. Egoism emphasizes self-interested motives; well, it seems clear that to have any chance of living a really satisfactory life we have to behave morally. Utilitarianism emphasizes the rights and interests of others; and if we have concern for others we'll behave morally towards them. I have my reservations about natural law theories of ethics, but they do seem right in pointing out a sort of essential morality in human nature."

Bowman paused and puffed on his pipe. "Then there are religious justifications for moral behavior. I'm an agnostic myself, but a genuine agnostic, not just a timid atheist. For all I know there may be a religious basis for morality. Perhaps with your Irish background you have thoughts on that, Miss Kelly?" Midge bit her lip and made no answer. Her ideas about religion were highly confused and highly personal, and she had no desire to expose them to Professor Bowman's coolly analytic eye. He may have guessed that, for his smile became even blander as he passed his fingers through his already rumpled hair and leaned back in his chair. "Plenty of reasons, Miss Kelly, take your pick. But so far as reasons which would cause whoever is displeasing you at the moment to behave better, I'm afraid I can't help you. I don't give personal advice."

For once Midge had the last word. As she gathered her purse and books she gave Bowman her sweetest smile and said, "That's good, Professor, because if you did I wouldn't take it." And she walked briskly out of the office, leaving Bowman for once looking less bland than usual.

This story raises several points. The first is the extent to which the study of philosophical ethics can be applied to practical problems. The second problem raised is the extent to which moral philosophy can give us reasons for moral behavior. And finally, there is the question of the extent to which a moral philosopher can be regarded as an expert on moral problems or a source of advice on such problems.

The distinction between theoretical and practical is relevant to all three questions. There is a difference between grasping the principles in a given area and being able to apply those principles in a specific case. Of course, it is possible to exaggerate this difference; the theoretician can benefit from practical experience, and the practical man can be helped by theory. But it is true that while a political scientist may know a great deal about the principles of government, an experienced politician may do better at achieving a given result.

The difficulty with theoretical knowledge is that it is general, and the solution of particular problems usually calls for detailed knowledge of facts. On the other hand, knowledge attained purely by practice and experience is often not general enough; it can be hard to teach to others and hard to apply to new situations. The political scientist might be less effective than the experienced politician on the politician's home ground, but if both had to understand and work with a political system in a foreign country, the political scientist, with his general grasp of the principles of government, might do much better than the politician deprived of familiar contacts and familiar wires to pull.

So an ethical theory which gives theoretical principles of conduct may seem to be of less use than "common sense" or "a good upbringing" in familiar cases. In dealing with family or friends, good habits may seem to be enough. But faced with new and puzzling situations, with problems about organ transplants or test-tube babies, we have to go back to basic principles. Consider the example given by Midge Kelly in our story: The principle "Do not harm others" seems general and abstract. But when we drive an automobile, carelessness or inattentiveness could lead to killing or mutilating another human being, and that is a matter of great practical importance. Similarly, any moral principle will necessarily be general and seem abstract, but there are plenty of quite practical and down-to-earth cases in which the application of moral principles such as "Keep commitments," "Repay benefactors," "Help others," and so on, is quite clear.

Consider now the question of how to justify or recommend moral behavior. Certainly a variety of arguments can be given. We can appeal to self-interest by urging that behavior which breaks moral rules will in the long run lead to unhappiness and harm to the person who acts in this way. The religious believer will want to consider rewards and punishments after death as well as satisfaction or dissatisfaction in this life. But, as we have seen before, there are limits to the appeal to self-interest. Some people want their own way more than they want joy or peace of mind. And if morality is pursued only for self-interested reasons, it ceases to be morality.

For persons of goodwill, who want the happiness and welfare of others, the moral philosopher can point out that treating others kindly and fairly and not harming them is the spelling out in practical detail of "goodwill towards men." He can argue from experience that mere goodwill is empty unless it is worked out in actions which are in accordance with moral rules. But a good many philosophers would be dissatisfied with any of the reasons for moral behavior we have given so far. They would want to say that morality must be recognized as something good in itself, not just as a means to other good things. In fact some philosophers—Kant, for instance—have argued that the only moral actions are those that are done just because the action is right. We will consider that point in a moment, but first let us look at the question of whether morality in itself is a motive for action.

On the face of it, morality does seem to be an independent motive for action. If I ask someone why he did something, several kinds of answers can be regarded as "final" or ultimate. If someone says, "I did it because it benefited me," that seems to answer the question "Why did you do it?" in a final way. So does an answer like "I did it to benefit X" where X is the name of another person. But we can also say, "I did it because it was right," and that also seems to be a final answer to the question "Why did you do it?"

In saying these are final answers I do not mean that *no* further question arises. We can ask, "What makes you think *that* benefited you?" or "How do you think *that* will benefit X?" or "What made you think *that* was right?" But "it benefited me," "it benefited X," and "it was right" all seem to give *adequate reasons* for doing the action referred to.

Contrast these answers with "I did it in order to make it bluer (larger, heavier, farther apart, etc.)." Any answer of this kind leaves open a further question: "But why did you want to do *that?*" On the other hand, "But why did you want to benefit yourself?" doesn't seem to make sense. "Why did you want to benefit *him?*" makes sense if there is some reason why you should not want to benefit that particular individual, but "Why benefit anyone else" seems just to be an expression of ethical egoism. Similarly, "Why do it because it's right?" is either puzzling or is a way of expressing ethical skepticism of some kind.

But this, we may feel, is not enough. Morality stands in need of some sort of foundation, or else the moral skeptic has a point. For if morality is without a foundation, surely the moral skeptic needs no more than this fact to show that moral skepticism is justified.

One possible answer to this is that moral skepticism is misguided in asking for a foundation for morality; morality is not in need of any support but is itself basic and fundamental. Just as sense perception is a source of knowledge which does not need to be based on anything else, so our moral knowledge does not need to be based on anything else. However, as we have seen, there are serious difficulties in comparing moral knowledge to sense perception; our knowledge of right and wrong is in the form of judgments rather than in the form of perception.

Perhaps, then, we should say that our knowledge of moral principles is like our knowledge of self-evident truths. We can see that $2 \times 2 = 4$ without having to base this knowledge on anything else; perhaps we can also see, for example, that wanton killing is wrong without having to base this knowledge on anything else. Probably the most plausible view of this kind is the view that it is the basic truths of morality which are thus self-evident and our judgments about particular cases come from applying these basic truths to these particular cases. A view very like this has been held by many ethical intuitionists, and such a view seems in many ways to do justice to our actual moral experience.

Such a view is especially plausible if we take the position that it is what is *prima facie* obligatory that is self-evident; we intuit the kinds of things that are morally *relevant,* not (directly) what is right or wrong. Surely to see that the fact that an action causes pain is *relevant* to its rightness or wrongness, whereas the fact that an action is done on Tuesday is not in itself relevant to its rightness or wrongness, is to see something so basic that it neither can be supported by anything else nor needs to be supported by anything else.

I have considerable sympathy for this line of argument, but I think that there are two difficulties with it. The first difficulty has to do with the fact that a pure intuitionist—Ross, for example—needs to call on intuition not only to know what is morally relevant but also to see which morally relevant consideration has most weight in a particular case. Or to put it in Ross's terminology, we need intuition not only to see what our *prima facie* obligations are, but to see which of several conflicting *prima facie* obligations is our strict obligation in a given case. This puts a considerable burden on the notion of "intuition," which is by no means clear in the first place. We would like, if possible, to see *why* our intuitions are as they are.

The second difficulty is the action-guiding aspect of moral rules. Moral principles seem in some way to support or imply imperatives such as "Do this!" "Don't do that!" This marks an important difference between moral principles and, say, mathematical or logical principles, which seem to say what is true but which do not seem to tell us what to do. In fact, the resemblance of moral principles to commands or requests has given rise to a moral theory known as *prescriptivism.* The word "prescription" is a useful general term for action-guiding utterances—commands, requests, advice, and so on. A prescriptivist moral theory says that moral principles are, or at least are similar to, universal prescriptions.

The simplest kind of prescriptivism simply says that moral principles *are* prescriptions; e.g., "It is wrong to steal" just means "I tell you not to steal." More sophisticated theories, like that of Richard Hare,[1] emphasize the importance of moral principles being accepted or approved by the person to whom moral statements are addressed; very roughly, in a theory like Hare's, "You ought not to steal" or "Stealing is wrong" becomes more like "I advise you not to steal, on the basis of an action-guiding principle which you yourself accept (or would accept if you were consistent)."

Either simple prescriptivism or Hare's version have some serious problems when they attempt to answer the question, "Why should I accept this advice?" Simple prescriptivism has to say either that prescriptions are unsupported, or that they are supported. Unsupported advice can be ignored, but to offer support for advice involves going beyond prescriptivism. Hare attempts to build in a reference to principles accepted by the person to whom the prescription is addressed. Suppose, however, that the person to whom you are saying that stealing is wrong rejects the principle on which your prescription is based. Hare attempts to show that in most cases the person would be inconsistent, for he will object to being stolen from himself. However, Hare admits that if the person *consistently* holds some odd moral principle, this theory has no reply. If, for example, I hold that anyone who breaks a promise should be killed, *including myself* if *I* break a promise, Hare would classify me as a "fanatic," and he admits that his theory cannot show that the fanatic is wrong.

Thus prescriptivist theories have serious drawbacks, but they do em-

[1] See R. M. Hare, *The Language of Morals* (Oxford: Oxford University Press, 1952).

phasize an important point—the action-guiding character of moral principles. A much more plausible theory, put forward by Robert Fogelin,[2] analyzes a statement such as "You ought not to steal" or "It is wrong to steal" as a statement that there are *good reasons* for the prescription "Don't steal!" This can easily be given a Rossian twist, so "You ought not to steal that money" becomes "The weight of morally relevant considerations is in favor of the prescription 'Don't steal that money!' " This has the advantage of making an "ought" statement the kind of utterance which can be true or false (whereas prescriptions cannot be either true or false), but at the same time showing how "ought" statements justify or imply prescriptions. But it brings to a head the problem raised earlier, for a statement like "The weight of morally relevant considerations is in favor of the prescription 'Do X' " does not look like a statement which can be in any obvious way "self-evident" or "logically true."

We can see, then, that one way of looking at the question of whether morality has a foundation is to regard it as a way of asking, "Why are certain considerations morally relevant and how do they support prescriptions?" Put in this way the question reminds us of questions in other areas of philosophy—for example: "How do sense perceptions support statements about material objects?" "How does information about the past and present support predictions about the future?" "How do the premises of a valid deductive argument support the conclusion?" All of these are questions about how one kind of statement can support or give evidence for another. In the moral case the question is especially acute because what is supported is a prescription and what is doing the supporting does not, at least on the face of things, look like prescriptions.

This is, of course, a new version of the question, "How can we get an 'ought' out of an 'is'?" The new version is, "How can we get a prescription from premises which are not prescriptions?" One way of solving the problem is to deny that the premises are not prescriptions—to say, as Hare and the other prescriptivists do, that moral principles are (or in some sense include) prescriptions. But of course if that were true then there would be no question of moral principles being self-evidently true or logically true, for prescriptions are neither true nor false (if you doubt this, try to assign a value of "true" or "false" to such typical prescriptions as "Shut the door," "Please sit down," "Don't waste your time on that book").

I have already suggested a possible answer to this problem in earlier discussions: the links between statements of fact and prescriptions are human wants and needs. The simplest case is the "hypothetical impera-

[2] In *Experience and Meaning* (London: Routledge & Kegan Paul, 1962).

tive." For example: You want to get to Australia quickly and comfortably (fact). Flying Qantas is the best way to get to Australia quickly and comfortably (fact). Conclusion: Fly Qantas! (prescription). Or we can say, "You *ought* to fly Qantas," which justifies the prescription "Fly Qantas," but says more than the prescription does because the "ought" is a signal that the prescription is not arbitrary but *justified.*

Moral cases, as was suggested earlier, differ from hypothetical imperatives because basic human needs are involved, not just wants or desires. But even in the hypothetical imperative cases there is something analogous to the relation between premises and conclusion in a deductive argument. The facts that I want A and that B is the best or only means to A justify or support the prescription "Do B!" If I change my mind about wanting A, or if B for some reason is no longer the best means to A, then the prescription "Do B!" is no longer justified. But if my wants do not change and B remains the best means to A, then the prescription "Do B!" must be regarded as justified.

Of course if I have *conflicting* desires A and Z and if B will bring about A but prevent Z, then the status of "Do B!" is no longer clear-cut. This case corresponds to conflicting *prima facie* obligations in the moral case, and the solution is similar: decide which is my *strongest* desire and then do whatever is the means to attaining that desire.

In the moral case we can see that the basis for the ranking of the Ross Rules is the extent to which the need served is more or less basic. The rule "Do not harm" is ranked highest because being harmed would prevent satisfaction of other needs. The rule "Keep commitments" is ranked higher than the rule "Help others," because our need to rely on commitments is more basic than our need for unsolicited help, and so on.

We are now in a position to see why "Because it is right to do X" or "Because I ought (morally) to do X" is (if true) a conclusive answer to the question, "Why should I do X?" Someone who agrees that it is right to do X is thereby agreeing that the weight of the morally relevant considerations favors the prescription "Do X!" To then ask, "But why should I do X?" is logically inconsistent with the acceptance of the premise "It is right to do X" or "I ought (morally) to do X." To reject the prescriptive "Do X!" is either to reject the premise "I ought to do X," or else to be logically inconsistent.

However, there are sensible questions that can be asked about the premise "It is right to do X" when it is interpreted as "The weight of morally relevant considerations is in favor of the prescription 'Do X!' " You can agree on what considerations are morally relevant, but ask to be shown that all morally relevant considerations have been taken into account and that the balance is indeed in favor of the prescription "Do X!" If this can be done then you would be willing to accept the prescription "Do X!" This kind of case is analogous to granting the evidential value of perception, but asking whether our perceptions justify us in a particular case in accepting a statement about a material object. Or again, it is analogous to accepting the ordinary standards for the verification of a scientific hypothesis, but wondering if in a particular case these standards have been applied correctly. In such cases we have a *practical* doubt about whether accepted standards have been correctly applied.

But we may also have a philosophical doubt about the ordinary standards—either a skeptical doubt about whether *any* standards are justified, or a theoretical doubt as to whether the standards we use are the best or only ones. The account given earlier of how the Ross Rules which specify *prima facie* duties (i.e., morally relevant considerations) are based on human needs for communication, acceptance and cooperation, love, friendship, and affection, gives a theoretical basis which enables us to see why we have the standards we do. Many philosophers have seen this to some extent, though not all have realized its essential place in the foundations of morality.

John Hospers, for example, discusses some of the answers given by Plato to the question, "Why obey moral principles?"

> First of all, according to Plato, it pays to live a just life because only in that way can you have the respect of your neighbors and friends—in fact only in that way can you *have* any friends. If you are not a trustworthy person who pays his debts and keeps his promises, other people will not trust you and will cease to have dealings with you. If you are trustworthy you will earn the respect and esteem of those around you. Therefore if you expect others to do decently by you, you would be wise to behave decently toward them. Only if you give will you also receive. Here, surely, is a perfectly sensible reason for being moral, a reason that will appeal strongly to most people. In fact it is probably the main reason in practice why people are moral.[3]

Hospers goes on to say that Plato did not give central importance to this kind of motivation for morality, and Hospers himself does not return to the point. But surely if he is right in saying that this is "the main reason in practice why people are moral," it deserves more careful discussion and a more central place in the discussion of the justification of moral action.

That such considerations have not been given a more central place is due, I think, to several causes. For one thing, our social and personal needs

[3] *Human Conduct* (New York: Harcourt Brace and World Inc., 1961).

are not always recognized as being as valid as our physical needs. For another thing, it is obvious that hypocrisy or money or power can enable us to obtain some degree of acceptance or cooperation, and less obvious that our real social and personal needs are not satisfied by the kind of acceptance or cooperation we can receive in these ways. The point is clearer with regard to our personal needs; friendship or love which can be secured by trickery or by money more clearly suffers by comparison with the real thing.

Morality, then, in some sense rests on human nature, or human needs, which are a part of human nature. But does human nature in turn depend on something else? For the humanist the answer must be "no"; human needs and human aspirations are, for him, ultimate. The religious believer will want to found morality ultimately on the nature of God, and will try to argue that founding morality on human nature is an inadequate basis for morality. To settle this dispute is beyond the scope of this book.

There may be a kind of moral skeptic who will still be unsatisfied by all we have said about the foundation of morality. He demands a *reason* for doing what is right or not doing what is wrong. There are several possible confusions here. If we are speaking from *within* a moral point of view, "this is right" *is* a reason, and a completely adequate reason, for doing it. If we reject moral justifications or reasons, we must be asking for some *nonmoral* reason for doing what is right and not doing what is wrong. But of course if there were, for example, a purely prudential reason for moral behavior, morality would be reduced to prudence, just as, if there were purely logical justifications for scientific laws, science would be reducible to logic.

The skeptic, of course, is up to his familiar tricks here; he is asking for the impossible and complaining because he can't get it. It is no more an objection to morality that we cannot give nonmoral reasons for doing what is (morally) right and not doing what is (morally) wrong, than it is an objection to science that we cannot give nonscientific justifications for scientific theories. In both cases we can raise second-order questions about why we have the standards we do, but these can be answered.

In general, the best reply to the moral skeptic, as to other skeptics, is to ask him what kind of answer would satisfy him. If, as is often the case, the ultimate answer is that *no* answer will satisfy the skeptic, then this in itself shows that we need not take the skeptic seriously. Questions with a built-in unanswerability are not serious questions.

But what about the practical problem of getting someone to act on the principle, "If it is right, do it; if it is wrong, don't do it"? Of course this is not one problem, but divides into a number of problems, depending on why the person wants to do wrong or refuses to do right. If the person is acting out of selfishness, we may need to bring in threats or rewards to wean him away from his self-centered behavior. If he refuses to act morally because of pity or excessive affection for someone, we can try to convince him that immoral behavior cannot really be in the interest of the other person.

But very often a person will behave immorally because he is convinced or confused by a false ethical theory. In such a case obviously Ethics can be a great deal of help.

What bearing does all this have on the question of whether teachers of Ethics will be good sources of moral advice? This question is complicated by the complicated nature of giving and receiving advice. I deliberately made Professor Bowman in the story a rather unattractive character. This unattractiveness is not irrelevant here, as it might be in the case of a competent doctor or lawyer. When we ask for moral advice, we want more than intellectual competence. Persons we ask for advice are usually people we respect and like or admire. To ask for advice is to put ourselves in a dependent and vulnerable position, and we do not like to do this with someone we dislike or distrust.

This is why it is always somewhat flattering to have your advice asked for, and somewhat insulting to have your advice rejected or spurned. In saying "I don't want your advice," Midge was telling Professor Bowman, "I don't respect you enough to ask your advice." And not to be respected is always a blow to the ego.

In concluding this book we must make clear what the study of Ethics can and cannot do. Clarity about ethical problems and about the basis of ethics can be valuable in itself, and valuable as an aid to moral action. But you can have complete intellectual clarity about ethical problems and still violate the principles you so clearly grasped. Knowledge influences the will, but it does not determine the will.

For the religious believer there are very powerful motives for moral behavior: gratitude, reverence, love of God, a feeling of the brotherhood of man under the fatherhood of God. The humanist will base his morality on love and respect for humanity as a whole, a feeling of unity with other humans in the face of a hostile universe. It is not the purpose of this book to decide which set of motives is more powerful or more based on reality (though I have very definite opinions on the matter).

Most people will find that they have need of some religious or quasi-religious (i.e., humanistic, Communist, etc.) motives for moral action. There will always be exceptional individuals for whom the mere fact that something is morally right provides all the motive they need to do that thing. But for most people it is unrealistic to expect this to be the *only* motive for moral behavior. Perhaps knowing a person of outstanding moral character gives a more powerful motive for ethical behavior than can be provided by the study of Ethics. But that does not mean that Ethics should not be studied. To paraphrase Kant, "Ethical knowledge without goodwill is barren, but goodwill without ethical knowledge is blind."

DISCUSSION QUESTIONS

1. Try to give a better answer to Midge Kelly's questions than that given by Professor Bowman.
2. To whom would you turn for moral advice? Why?
3. What factors motivate your own moral choices?
4. In what way are moral principles we have discussed relevant to decisions you make in everyday life?
5. How has a course in Ethics or reading about Ethics affected your own moral thinking?
6. Which ethical theory are you now inclined to favor?
7. Have you changed your moral opinions as the result of taking a course on Ethics or reading about Ethics? In what way? What arguments impressed you?
8. In this book, what part or aspect (if any) did you think especially good? Why? What part or aspect (if any) did you think especially bad? Why?
9. Try to state the moral code (if any) by which you live.
10. What actions that your moral code requires of you are you not doing? What do you intend to do about it?

FURTHER READINGS

FRANKENA, WILLIAM, *Ethics* (2nd ed.). Englewood Cliffs, N.J.: Prentice-Hall, Inc., 1973.

FRANKENA, WILLIAM, and JOHN GRANROSE, *Introductory Readings in Ethics.* Englewood Cliffs, N.J.: Prentice-Hall, Inc., 1974:

FINDLAY, J. N., "Ethical Judgments and Their Justification," pp. 438-451

NEILSEN, KAI, "On Moral Truth," pp. 451-467.

WARNOCK, G. J., "The Concept of Morality," pp. 467-471.

SELLARS, WILFRED, and JOHN HOSPERS, *Readings in Ethical Theory.* (2nd ed.). New York: Appleton-Century-Crofts, 1970:

HOSPERS, JOHN, "Why Be Moral," pp. 730-747.

NEILSEN, KAI, "Why Should I Be Moral," pp. 747-767.

Additional Suggested Readings

INTRODUCTION TO ETHICS

GEISLER, NORMAN, *Ethics, Issues and Alternatives.* Grand Rapids, Mich.: Zondervan Publishers Co., 1972.

GERT, BERNARD, *The Moral Rules.* New York: Harper & Row, 1970.

HOSPERS, JOHN, *Human Conduct* (shorter ed.). New York: Harcourt Brace Jovanovich, 1972.

WELLMAN, CARL, *Morals and Ethics.* Glenview, Ill.: Scott, Foresman and Co., 1975.

STUDIES IN ETHICAL THEORY

BRANDT, RICHARD B., *Ethical Theory.* Englewood Cliffs, N.J.: Prentice- Hall, Inc., 1959.

ROSS, W. D., *The Right and the Good.* Oxford: Oxford University Press, 1930.

———, *Foundations of Ethics.* Oxford: Oxford University Press, 1937.

TOULMIN, STEPHAN, *The Place of Reason in Ethics.* Cambridge: Cambridge University Press, 1960.

WARNOCK, G. J., *Contemporary Moral Philosophy.* New York: St. Martin's Press, 1967.

ANTHOLOGIES: ETHICAL THEORIES

Davis, Philip E., *Introduction to Moral Philosophy*. Columbus, Ohio: Charles E. Merrill Publishing Co., 1973.

Ekman, Roselind, *Readings in the Problems of Ethics*. New York: Charles Scribner's Sons, 1965.

Foot, Phillipa, *Theories in Ethics*. Oxford: Oxford University Press, 1967.

Sellars, Wilfred, and John Hospers, *Readings in Ethical Theory*. New York: Appleton-Century-Crofts, 1970.

ANTHOLOGIES: ETHICAL PROBLEMS

Beck, Robert N., and John B. Orr, *Ethical Choice*. New York: The Free Press, 1970.

Durland, William R., and William H. Bruening, *Ethical Issues*. Palo Alto, Calif.: Mayfield Publishing Company, 1975.

Girvetz, Harry K., *Contemporary Moral Issues*. Belmont, Calif.: Wadsworth Publishing Co., 1963.

Appendix: A Capsule History Of Ethics

INTRODUCTION

Knowing the history of a subject is always of some help in understanding that subject; how much help it is varies from subject to subject. Usually in philosophy it is considerably helpful to know something about the history of a question or set of questions, because philosophy is in many ways like a debate or discussion going on through the ages. Just as we are puzzled if we come into the middle of a discussion or debate without knowing who has said what or what arguments have been used, so we are likely to be puzzled if we begin to study a philosophical problem without knowing anything of its history.

However, just as a brief summary of the discussion so far may be enough to get us launched into an argument or debate, so also a brief summary of the history of ethics may be enough to start us off on the study of ethics. When we have gotten some idea of the pros and cons of various positions and have formed some opinions of our own, we may want to go back to a more detailed study of the history of the subject, to discover more about various views and why people have found them convincing. This Appendix gives a brief introduction to or summary of the history of ethics and should be supplemented by other reading as your interests and opportunities allow.

A very important thing to remember at the beginning of any historical study is that the same subject can be different in important ways at different periods. For example, the theory of government always has to do with how people can live together in communities, but at one time the rights and responsibilities of hereditary monarchs was an important part of the theory of government, whereas today there are few kings or queens and their importance is small. Still, unless we understand the debates about the powers of monarchy which went on in past centuries we will not understand properly, for example, the differences between Canadian and American views of government.

In the history of ethics the first thing to realize is that although ethics has always been concerned with right and wrong, good and bad, different questions have been asked about these at different times. Thus the Greeks and Romans before the spread of Christianity had a different approach to ethics than did Europeans in the Middle Ages or at the time of the Reformation. So there are always three questions to ask about a historical ethical theory:

1. What question was this theory trying to answer?
2. What answer does this theory give to that question?
3. How is this answer related to our contemporary ethical problems and concerns?

In this Appendix I try to answer these questions for some of the major historical schools of ethics. It is important to realize that a short survey of the history of ethics must necessarily concentrate on a broad overview and omit details and qualifications. So such a survey is bound to be overgeneral and oversimplified. A map shows you the main features and their relationships: it is not a substitute for a visit to the territory in question. A survey like this is no substitute for a complete history of ethics or for an acquaintance with the original sources. At the end of this Appendix are some suggested readings in the history of ethics. You should go to them not only for further information but also for different views of the history of ethics: you yourself must arrive at a balanced view by your own understanding and judgment.

I. CLASSICAL ANTIQUITY

Greece: General Tendencies. Men were thinking about ethical problems long before the civilizations of Greece and Rome, but for an understanding of present-day ethical thinking in countries with a European heritage the first major influence we need to consider is that of these two great Mediterranean nations. For a variety of reasons the Greek approach to ethics was intellectual rather than emotional, philosophical rather than religious, and moderate rather than extreme. For the Greeks, the main question of ethics was "How can I live the good life?" and by "the good life" they meant primarily a happy or satisfactory life.

The Sophists. The first attempts to answer this kind of question were by a group of philosophers we now lump together as "The Sophists." The term "Sophist" literally means "wise man," but it was used by critics of the Sophists in an unfavorable sense (as in the obsolete slang terms "wise guy" or "wiseacre") meaning really "someone who pretends to be wise." The Sophists gave the same kind of answers to the question "How can I live a good life?" which often come up in present-day discussions: "You can live a good life by being successful," where by success some Sophists meant political power, others money, others a life of physical pleasure. Many of the Sophists claimed to be able to teach others how to be successful, and charged money for their instruction. Some of them were probably only clever confidence men, but others may have done their clients some good, if only by giving them self-assurance.[1] (Much the same can be said of present-day teachers of lessons in salesmanship or courses on "how to win friends and influence people.")

Socrates. The history of ethics really begins when Socrates (470–399 B.C.) began to think philosophically about the problems of ethics. Socrates was probably the first person to carry on the activity of clarifying, criticizing, and arguing about fundamental problems which we now call philosophy. In the area of ethics Socrates raised questions about what the good life really was and how we could attain it. If success was really what we meant by a good life, then why didn't more people admire the successful tyrant or philanderer, and why did successful people often seem dissatisfied? Socrates raised many more questions than he answered; probably the closest he came to having an ethical position of his own was his conviction that if we could only discover what the good life *was*, we would be bound to try to attain it. Socrates thought of evil-doing as a sort of ignorance of our own best interests: if we had knowledge of the good we would be bound to live according to it.

Plato. Socrates' greatest pupil, Plato (427–347 B.C.), gave his own answers to some of the questions Socrates had raised. Plato saw man as a sort of composite, composed of intellect, emotions, and appetites. For Plato the way to live a good life was to bring emotions and appetites under the control of intellect. He thought of the imperfect, changing world revealed to us by our senses as a sort of image or copy of a perfect, un-

[1] Some present-day scholars would give a much more favorable estimate of the Sophists, but this is the generally accepted view.

changing ideal world, so that for intellect to control the appetites and emotions meant that we would attempt to conform our actions to ideal justice and goodness. But since Plato saw the practices and stereotypes of his society as universally valid, this meant in practice that virtue for a slave was to serve his master, virtue for a wife was to be docile and submissive. Only the adult, male, free citizen could exercise choice and initiative, and he in turn had his role to play in supporting and defending the state.

Aristotle. Aristotle (384–322 B.C.) was a pupil of Plato but came to disagree with him on many things. He rejected Plato's idea of a separate ideal world and saw universal principles as embodied in concrete cases, existing separately only in our minds. Aristotle saw the good life as a life of *doing*, a life of activity governed by good principles. In explaining what he meant by good principles, Aristotle made the Greek admiration for moderation into a theory: the doctrine of the Golden Mean. He argued that every good principle of action is a mean or balance between two extremes. Courage, for example, is a mean between the two extremes of rashness and cowardice. Cowardice pays too much attention to danger, rashness too little; courage pays just enough attention to danger and is thus the "mean" between rashness and cowardice; the "balanced" attitude towards danger.

Other Schools. Plato and Aristotle both founded schools of philosophy, predecessors of our modern universities and colleges. Other philosophers as well, many of them thinking of themselves as carrying on what Socrates had begun, founded their own schools of philosophy. Some of these philosopher's had far more popular influence than Plato or Aristotle, though most philosophers see them as less important for the development of ethics.

Epicureans and Stoics. Two important views of ethics in the later classical period were the school founded by Epicurus (342–270 B.C.), and a group of philosophers who were called "Stoics" because their meeting place in Athens was a colonnade or porch (*stoa* in Greek). The Epicureans held a more sophisticated version of the popular view that the good life was a life of pleasure. But far from recommending a life of wild sensual indulgence, the Epicureans taught that the mental pleasures of study and friendship were far longer-lasting and had fewer bad side effects than sensual pleasures like eating or sexual intercourse. (Also, they said, mental pleasures are considerably cheaper!) But basically the Epicureans thought that getting as much pleasure as possible (and as little pain as possible) was the formula for a good life. In matters not directly related to individual pain or pleasure the Epicureans recommended conformity to whatever customs were practiced by the society you lived in.

The Stoics, on the other hand, held that the way to have a satisfactory life was to have as few wants and desires as possible and to live in accordance with nature. They would distinguish between natural desires like those for food or warmth, and desires which went beyond nature like a desire for gourmet foods or an elaborate mansion. The Stoics thought that the family was a "natural" institution, so they recommended good citizenship and care for one's family. But they rejected slavery and the conquest of one people by another as unnatural and thought of all men as brothers and fellow "citizens of the universe." This gave Stoicism a wide appeal among men of goodwill in all classes: two famous Stoics were Epictetus, who started life as a slave, and Marcus Aurelius, a Roman emperor.

Both Stoicism and Epicureanism appealed to the Romans: Epicureanism to their luxury-loving side and Stoicism to their serious, responsible side. Many of the "dropouts" from Roman society, the sensual and irresponsible aristocrats and their hangers-on, thought of themselves as Epicureans, while Stoicism became almost an official religion among the serious-minded rulers and administrators of the Roman Empire. However, the ordinary Roman citizen during the later Empire was often morally confused; the philosophical theories of morality were too abstract for him, the traditional values of Roman society seemed to be no longer valid. Romans turned in great numbers to "mystery religions" from the Near East, and the moral vacuum in which they lived made many citizens of the later Empire ready and eager to embrace Christianity when it appeared.

Classical Ethics and Modern Problems. Two points ought to be remembered in connection with ethics in the Classical period. First, I have emphasized what is distinctive in this period rather than what is common to Classical ethics and later ethics. The Classical period had its ethical skeptics and relativists; some of the Sophists' theories had elements of ethical egoism and some elements of Plato's or Aristotle's theories resemble utilitarian or rule theories. But the differences in approach are important since they put these elements in a different perspective.

Second, we can note that questions about how to live the good life, in the sense meant by the Greeks and Romans, are no longer a central issue in ethics. Many present-day ethical theorists would regard this question as outside their concerns, although a few contemporary books on ethics discuss these or related problems. However, perhaps this attitude means that important questions of value are no longer being subjected to philosophical analysis and examination. The question of how best to live a happy and satisfactory life is certainly one which is still of concern to people, and it is still discussed at "bull sessions" and in popular books and articles. One advantage of learning about the history of ethics is that it frees us from a narrow concentration on the problems which seem important to our own times and gives us a wider perspective on the questions which have seemed important to other ages and cultures.

II. JUDEO-CHRISTIAN ETHICS

General Tendencies. The Jewish culture, within which Christianity arose, was very different from that of Greece and Rome. Jewish ethical views were founded on divine revelation rather than on philosophical speculation. They were in sharp contrast to the prevailing ethical views of the cultures around them and for this reason seemed harsh and extreme to those outside Judaism. Jewish, and later Christian, ethics was based on God rather than man, and on a revealed code of behavior rather than on philosophical speculation about the good life. For Judeo-Christian ethics the primary questions was, "How can I be in the right relation with God?" rather than "How can I live the good life?" Being in the right relation with God included a hope that God would reward and recompense his faithful followers, either in this life or in an afterlife; but for the devout Jew or Christian, loving and serving God was more important than the hope of reward.

Jewish Ethics. Jews and Christians could agree that serving God included obeying His commandments and knowing Him more deeply. As Judaism and Christianity developed over a period of history, the distinctively Jewish interpretation of this common ground came to differ more sharply from the Christian interpretation. Judaism emphasized a minute observance of the Mosaic law, both ethical and ceremonial, and a careful study of the Torah and the commentaries on it. Thus a "good Jew" came to mean someone who not only kept the Ten Commandments, but also observed dietary and ceremonial law, as well as devoting what time he could to the study of Torah and commentary or at least supporting and respecting those who could.

Catholic and Protestant Interpretations of Christian Ethics. At the Protestant reformation two tendencies in Christian ethics became sharply separated. Protestants emphasized the importance of faith and the experience of conversion or commitment to God, while Catholics emphasized the doing of good works and the training of our wills in submission to God. It is easy to exaggerate the differences between the Protestant and Catholic views; for the Protestant, good works were the natural result of, and a sign of, conversion to God, whereas for the Catholic, good works without faith and the help of God were useless. But the Protestant ideal of the good man tended to emphasize conversion—a vital and often dramatic experience of "accepting Christ"; the Catholic ideal (as shown, for example, in lives of saints) emphasized penitential practices for the training of the will and works of devotion or charity. John Wesley might be a good example of the Protestant ideal, St. Francis of Assisi a good example of the Catholic ideal.

Judeo-Christian Ethics and Modern Problems. The tendency of Judaism and Christianity in their various forms was to emphasize the brotherhood of man under the fatherhood of God; this led to major social and political changes in European society. If most people of European heritage now assume that each human being is a person worthy of respect, that the strong should help the weak or that hatred and vindictiveness are evil, this attitude is largely due to the influence of Judaism and Christianity. None of these things would have seemed obvious, or even true, to a Greek or Roman in the Classical period, nor do they now seem obvious or true to members of non-Western civilizations uninfluenced by Judaism or Christianity. The idea of love of God and love of neighbor as the essence of morality is perhaps the distinctive element of Judeo-Christian morality, which distinguishes it from pre-Judeo-Christian and contemporary non-Judeo-Christian morality.

The present-day importance of the Judeo-Christian approach to morality will depend largely, but not entirely, on the extent to which some form of Jewish or Christian religious belief and practice is accepted. For the practicing Jew or Christian the morality which is part of his religion will be the morality he will try to live by. But the sympathetic atheist or humanist who has rejected Jewish or Christian religious beliefs can see value in the approach to morality found in Judaism or Christianity. Such a person will presumably try to extract what lessons he can from the moral teachings of Jewish or Christian religious teachers, while rejecting the religious framework in which they occur. Whether this is really possible, whether you can have Judeo-Christian morality, or even part of it, without its theological foundations is a matter of dispute between believers and nonbelievers.

III. SECULAR ETHICS

A. The British Tradition

We can distinguish from Judeo-Christian morality, secular moralities no doubt influenced by Christianity in some respects, but not based on the Jewish or Christian revelations. Most of these arose after the Reformation and its consequent religious disagreements had weakened Christianity. It will be convenient to separate secular moralities into those in the tradition of British empiricism and those in the Continental rationalist tradition. Though there are sharp disagreements within these traditions, there is enough similarity to make this division useful.

British Ethics: General Tendencies. Ethical theories developed in the British Isles tended to appeal to experience rather than to pure reason; there are some notable exceptions, but this empiricism element is strongly marked in British ethical writers. For these writers, "How should I treat my fellow human beings?" became the central question of morality, rather than "How can I live the good life?" or "How can I be in the right relation to God?" The focus had changed from our relation to God to our relation with our fellow men, from the satisfactory life for the individual to problems of social interaction.

Hobbes. Thomas Hobbes (1588–1679) was the first important British secular moralist. Hobbes was both a psychological and an ethical egoist (see Chapter 2) and thought that the answer to the question of how we should treat our fellow human beings was, "Treat them in such a way as to protect yourself from them and to gain their cooperation." Hobbes thought that without organized society there would be constant warfare of one individual against another, each seeking to dominate and enslave others while protecting himself. To avoid this constant warfare, which would make life "nasty, brutish, and short" it was reasonable, on purely self-interested grounds, to join together in organized society where each individual gives up some of his freedom to have security and order. Thus for Hobbes, ethics became a sort of social engineering: How can I get the best return in security for the surrender of my freedom?

Hume. The next really new theory in British ethics was that of David Hume (1711–1776), who reversed Plato's idea that the intellect should rule the emotions and appetites, by arguing that intellect as such has no desires (Plato would have disagreed). Therefore, Hume argued, intellect can only plan out means to attain goals set by the "passions" (emotion and appetite). Thus Hume concluded that "reason both is and ought to be the slave of the passions." However, altruistic emotions and desire for approval are part of human nature as Hume saw it, so that his theory, though basically egoistic, allowed a place for benevolent actions. Hume's answer to the basic question, then, was: "You should treat human beings in such a way as to satisfy your passions, including your altruistic or benevolent passions." In discussing which actions would achieve this best, Hume often seemed to anticipate utilitarian views.

Price and Reid. Hume's theory was objected to from an intuitionist point of view by Richard Price (1723–1791) and Thomas Reid (1710–

1796), whose views in many ways resembled those of W. D. Ross (see Chapter 4). Another theory popular around this time was a theory that human beings are endowed with a "moral sense" not unlike our senses of taste, touch, etc., which enable us to discern good and evil. Depending on whether "moral sense" was interpreted as giving objective information or merely a subjective feeling, moral sense theories resembled either an intuitionism like that of Price and Reid or a theory like that of Hume.

Utilitarianism. The next important British ethical theory was utilitarianism, which is discussed in Chapter 3. The two important figures in early utilitarianism are Jeremy Bentham (1748–1832) and John Stuart Mill (1806–1873), who represent two different approaches to this theory. Bentham put forward the utilitarian principle, "the greatest good of the greatest number," as an all-sufficient basis of ethics: if common sense morality or the moral judgments of ordinary people differed from what would be required by the utilitarian principle, so much the worse for them. Mill, on the other hand, tried to modify utilitarianism to bring it closer to comomn-sense morality and the judgments we ordinarily make. Mill's claim was that utilitarianism was the clearest and most satisfactory theory for organizing and systematizing our everyday moral judgments. Henry Sidgwick (1838–1900) continued Mill's project of trying to show that utilitarianism was the theory that best fitted our common-sense ethical judgments, but conceded that utilitarianism must begin with a moral intuition of the truth of the utilitarian principle itself.

B. Continental Ethics

Spinoza. Philosophers on the continent of Europe at this period were also concerned with man rather than God and with social interaction rather than individual happiness. But in accordance with the general tendency of non-British European philosophy, reason rather than experience was emphasized. Benedict Spinoza (1632–1677) was, like Hobbes, both a psychological and ethical egoist, but he attempted to derive from basically egoistic premises a relatively humane, tolerant, and enlightened ethical view. Spinoza tried to treat ethics like Euclidean geometry, laying down axioms and definitions and attempting to derive more specific ethical judgments from principles of self-preservation and self-development.

Kant's Theory. The other great figures of Continental rationalism had little to say about ethics and it is not until we come to Immanuel Kant (1724–1804) that we find a striking European contribution to ethical theory. Kant attempted to derive a moral theory from an analysis of how any intelligent being must guide his conduct. He emphasized intentions rather than performance, and held that the only thing good without qualification was a good will, by which Kant meant a will that chose to do the right thing simply because it was right, not because of any advantage to oneself or others. Kant's answer to the question, "How shall I treat my fellow human beings" was that we should treat others as ends in themselves, and not as means to our own purposes—that we should act only on principles which we would be willing to see made universal laws. (This view is briefly discussed in Chapter 7.)

Other Ethical Theories. Other theories held by European philosophers outside of Britain were heavily influenced by Kant, but one independent ethical tradition was the idea of self-realization as the basis of ethics. Some thinkers, for example, Arthur Schopenhauer (1788–1860) and Friedrich Nietzsche (1844–1900), interpreted self-realization in a basically egoistic way, but others, especially G.W.F. Hegel (1770–1831) and his followers, thought of the self-realization of the individual as part of a process of development embracing the whole human race.

As can be seen from this brief survey, many of the ethical theories discussed in the first five chapters of this book were developed and argued in the period between the sixteenth and twentieth centuries. This was the period in which ethics was no longer based on religion, but in which primary attention was focused on questions of normative ethics rather than of meta-ethics. To a large extent we are still debating theories originated or developed during this period, and our basic question is still, "How should we behave toward our fellow human beings?" rather than "How can I be in the right relation to God?" or "How can I live the good life?"

IV. CONTEMPORARY ETHICAL THEORY

The early part of the twentieth century was preoccupied with meta-ethical questions, questions about the nature and foundations of morality. There was a sharp attack on the objectivity of ethics by philosophers who wanted to judge ethics by the standards of proof and justification used in mathematics and science. The most influential attacks of this kind came from A.J. Ayer (born 1910) in England and Charles Stevenson (born 1908) in the United States. Much of the subsequent discussion in the first fifty or sixty years of the century was an attempt to meet criticisms of this kind. G.E. Moore (1873–1958) developed an intuitionist theory in which just as yellow is a simple quality perceived by the senses, so good and bad are simple qualities perceived directly by moral intuition. Moore's theory was the starting point for much discussion during the first part of the century.

Probably the fatal blow to a simple intuitionism like Moore's was struck by R.M. Hare (born 1919), who pointed out that good and bad are not simple qualities; two chairs can be identical in every way except that one is yellow and the other is blue; but if two actions are identical in every way one cannot be good and the other bad. Thus good and bad are "supervenient" or "consequential" properties, not, as Moore thought, simple properties. Hare's own ethical theory was a highly sophisticated prescriptivism (briefly discussed in Chapter 10).

Other important theories about ethics put forward in the twentieth century were new and more sophisticated versions of both utilitarianism and intuitionism, especially the highly developed intuitionist theory of W.D. Ross (1877–1973) discussed in Chapter 4.

On the continent of Europe the aftermath of World War II brought existentialism to the fore; the ethical theories of the existentialists are in general a form of ethical individualism of the kind discussed in Chapter 5. Another form of ethical individualism was put forward by Joseph Fletcher (born 1905) partly in response to the moral ambiguities of the "cold war" era of the Fifties and Sixties.

Two recent developments in ethical theory are worth mentioning. The first is a new theory which is in some way like that of Hobbes: an attempt to argue for an organized society, with mutual rights and obligations, from basically egoistic premises. This theory is briefly discussed in Chapter 10; its contemporary version is due almost entirely to John Rawls (born 1921).

Another interesting development is the attempt to apply the formal techniques of mathematical logic to ethical questions. Two Scandinavians, George Henryk von Wright (born 1916) and Jaakko Hintikka (born 1929), have done some especially interesting work in this area. So far these attempts have given us little that is of interest for ethical theory, but "the logic of morals" or "mathematical ethics" is now beginning to develop to the extent that some fruitful interactions between ethics and logic may soon be possible.

Finally, it is worth noting that the exclusive concentration of philosophers on meta-ethics as opposed to normative ethics seems to be over as we enter the last quarter of the twentieth century. Articles and books on such ethical problems as war, abortion, racial discrimination, etc., are coming from professional philosophers, and perhaps even too little attention is being paid to meta-ethical issues. The tendency in many college and university courses in Ethics (as well as in textbooks such as this one) is now to give equal time to meta-ethics and normative ethics.

FURTHER READING

The first thing to read after this brief survey is probably a good encyclopedia article on the history of ethics. Articles in recent editions of good general encyclopedias such as the *Britannica* or *Americana* will be useful, but the best one is:

The Encyclopedia of Philosophy, Vol. 3, ed. Paul Edwards. New York: The Macmillan Company, 1967.

There are surprisingly few good introductions to the history of ethics. Two worth looking at are:

MacIntyre, Alastair, *A Short History of Ethics.* New York: The Macmillan Company, 1966.

Sidgwick, Henry, *Outlines of the History of Ethics.* London: Macmillan and Co., 1886, reprinted 1931.

There are a multitude of good books about specific periods in the history of ethics or specific ethical philosophers or theories. You might start with:

Broad, C. D., *Five Types of Ethical Theory.* New York: Harcourt Brace Jovanovich, 1930.

Hospers, John, *Human Conduct.* New York: Harcourt Brace Jovanovich, 1961.

A good selection of excerpts from the original writings of philosophers on ethical problems (in chronological order) is:

Jones, W. T., *et al., Approaches to Ethics.* New York: McGraw-Hill Book Company, 1962.

Finally, two excellent books on contemporary meta-ethics are:

Hudson, W. D., *Modern Moral Philosophy.* Garden City, N.Y.: Doubleday and Company (Anchor Books), 1970.

Warnock, G. J., *Contemporary Moral Philosophy.* New York: St. Martin's Press, 1967.

Subject Index

Abortion, 68, 69, 78, 79
Actions, 32
Advice, moral, 126
Altruistic behavior, 20, 21
Anthropology, 8–9

Balance of terror, 76
Bay of Pigs invasion, 73
Beneficence, 42
British ethics, 136–38

Capital punishment, 76–78
Categorical imperative, 85–86
Catholicism, 68, 135–36
Chinese culture, 69
Christianity, 23, 38, 70
Classical ethics, 131–34
Confederacy, 73
Commitment, personal, 85
Communism, 75
Conflict, ethical, 56–58
Conscience, 5, 63–65
Conscientious objection, 90
Contemporary ethics, 140–41
Continental ethics, 138–40
Contract theory, 112–13

Death penalty, 71, 77–78
Decent behavior, 20–21
Deontological theories, 13
Divine Glory theory, 10, 11, 12, 47
Divine Will theory, 9, 10, 11, 12, 14, 47
Duties, 42–45, 61, 108

Ecological ethics, 108–11, 113–14
Ecology, 109–10
Egoism:
  ethical, 10, 12, 18, 23, 24, 26, 38, 47, 65
  psychological, 10, 18, 22, 23, 26
Environment, 110
Environmental rights, 113–14

Ethics:
  British, 136–38
  classical, 131–34
  contemporary, 140–41
  continental, 138–40
  ecological, 108–11, 113–14
  Greek, 131–32
  history of, 130–41
  Jewish, 135
  meta-, viii, 139, 140
  normative, viii, 139
  practical, 118
  Roman, 131–32
  sexual, 88, 111
  situation, 11, 53, 55–57, 62–63
  theoretical, 118
Euthanasia, 69
Exploitation, 95

Fairness, 35, 36, 96, 112
Family, 88
Favoritism, 103
Fidelity, 42, 44
Fort Sumter, 73

God, 10, 11, 14, 24, 36, 47, 77, 83, 89, 111, 112
Goods, moral, 45–46
Greatest good, 28, 30, 31, 33, 35, 46
Greek ethics, 131–32
Greek philosophers, 23, 69
Gulf of Tonkin resolution, 73

Happiness, 19–20, 38
Harm, 58–62, 99–100
Hierarchical view, 56, 65
Homosexuality, 90
Human nature theory, 11, 12

Illegitimacy, 82
Imperative, categorical, 85–86
Imperative, hypothetical, 85–86, 122, 123
Individualism, ethical, 11, 12, 48, 51, 140
Intercourse, premarital, 84, 88
Intimacy, sexual, 82
Intuition, moral, 120–21
Intuitionism, 12, 24, 138, 139
Israeli-Arab conflict, 74
I–thou relationships, 86

Japanese society, 3–4
Jewish ethics, 135
Jewish people, 37, 74
Judeo-Christian:
  morality, 88, 135–36
  view of marriage, 83–84
Judgment, ethical, 47, 58

Killing, 69–72
  defensive, 71

Law, equality before, 95
Lesser evil, 72

Malicious behavior, 20, 21
Marriage, 82–83, 85
Medical profession, 69
Meta-ethics, viii, 139, 140
Minority groups, 94–95
Monogamy, 84
Monandry, 84
Morality, foundations of, 50–51, 119–27
Moral Philosophy, 3
Moral sense, 46–47
Motives for action, 119–20
My Lai massacre, 74

Naturalism, 12
Natural law theory, 11, 12, 82
Natural rights, 111–12
Nature, human, 48–49, 125
Nazis, 74–75
Needs, human, 48–49, 50, 125
Noncognitivism, 12, 25
Non-maleficence, 42
Non-naturalism, 12
Normative ethics, viii, 139

On, 3–4
Opportunity, 96–99, 102
Ought, and is, 122
  hypothetical, 49–50, 122–23
  instrumental, 49–50, 122–23

Pearl Harbor attack, 73
Person, 70–71
Pluralistic society, 90–91
Poland, 74
Pollution, 109–10
Polyandry, 84
Polygamy, 84
Population, 110–11
Practical ethics, 118
Pregnancy, 82
Prescriptivism, 121–23, 140
Prima facie obligation, 43, 56, 120, 123
Principles, moral, 120–21
Promiscuity, 83, 85–86
Protestantism, 11, 135–36
Punishment, capital (*see* Capital punishment)

Quotas, 102–3

Rape, 1–2
Relationships:
  personal, 85–88, 96
  premarital, 84–85
  sexual, 84–85
Relativism:
  cultural, 8–9, 12
  ethical, 8
  individual, 9
  social, 8–9, 12, 47
Reparation, 41, 43, 98–100, 104
Revised Ranked Ross Rules, 58–62
Rhodesia, 14
Rights:
  natural, 111
  and obligations, 108
Roman ethics, 131–32
Roman philosophers, 69
Ross rules, 49, 51, 63, 89, 95, 123, 124

Seduction, 83
Self-destructive behavior, 21
Selfish behavior, 21
Self-respect, 103
Self-serving behavior, 21
Self-torturing behavior, 21
Sexual ethics, 88, 111
Situation ethics, 11, 53, 55–57, 62–63
Skepticism, 25–26
Slavery, 34, 70
Sophists, 132
Spiteful behavior, 21
Stoicism, 11, 133–34
Subjectivism, 4–7, 9, 12, 13, 14, 47
Suicide, 89, 111

Tact, 87, 88
Teleological theories, 13
Theoretical ethics, 118
Tolerance, 6–8
Truth, 33

Unhappiness, 19–20
Utilitarianism, 10, 12, 28
  act, 31–32, 33, 65
  hedonistic, 30, 38
  ideal, 31, 32, 38, 46
  ranked rule, 33
  rule, 31, 32, 33, 38, 65

Vietnamese war (*see* War, Vietnamese)

War, 72–76
  Biafran, 74–75
  just, 72–76, 79
  Korean, 73
  Nigerian, 74
  Vietnamese, 2, 6, 72
Women, 83, 84

Index of Names

Note: Names of fictional characters are in italics.

Anscombe, G. E. M., 80
Aristotle, 48, 89, 132, 134
Aurelius, Marcus, 134
Ayer, A. J., 15, 139

Beauchamp, Thomas, 79, 92, 104, 115
Beck, Robert N., 129
Bedeau, Hugo, 79
Bentham, Jeremy, 34, 38, 138
Bertocci, Peter, 92
Blashard, Brand, 52
Bowman, Professor, 116–18, 126, 127
Boxill, Bernard R., 105
Brandt, Richard, 38, 80, 128
Broad, C. D., 15, 141
Brown, Harry, 40–41, 44–45
Brown, Tom, 40–41, 44–45
Bruening, William H., 129
Buber, Martin, 86
Buchan, Dr., 67–69, 79
Butler, Joseph, 27
Butler, Rev. Robert, 53–55, 65

Carritt, E. F., 66
Cicero, 15
Confucius, 89
Cratchit, Mrs., 56–57
Crozier, Rev. Carl, 53–55

Davis, Philip E., 129
Dick (Prince Peter's friend), 28–29
Dick (Tom Brown's friend), 41, 44–45
Devlin, Patrick, 92
Donagan, Alan, 28
Durland, William, 129

Ed, Dr., 40–41, 44–45
Edmund, Grand Duke, 30

Edwards, Joanna, 93–94, 104
Edwards, Paul, 141
Ekman, Rosalind, 129
Epictetus, 134
Epicurus, 133
Ewing, A. C., 15, 27, 38, 51, 66

Findlay, J. N., 127
Fletcher, Joseph, 53, 66
Flew, Antony, 79
Fogelin, Robert, 122
Foot, Phillipa, 129
Fotheringay, Mrs., 67–69, 70, 79
Francis of Assisi, St., 136
Frankena, William, 15, 27, 38, 52, 66, 127
Fredericks, Jimmy, 55
Fred Perkins, 1–3, 14

Garrigan, Mrs., 54
Geisler, Norman, 128
Gert, Bernard, 128
Givertz, Harry K., 129
Granrose, John, 15, 27, 38, 52, 66
Grisez, Germaine, 80

Hâre, Richard M., 121, 140
Harry, 2–3, 14
Harry Brown, 40–41, 44
Hart, H. L. A., 80, 92
Hegel, G. W. F., 139
Hintikka, Jaakko, 140
Hobbes, Thomas, 137
Holland, R. F., 80
Hospers, John, 27, 38, 124, 127, 128, 129, 141
Hudson, W. D., 141
Hughes, Graham, 104
Huxley, Aldous, 30

Jean Kane, 106–8, 115
Jimmy Fredericks, 55
Joanna Edwards, 93–94, 104
Johnson, Dewey, 94
Johnson, President Lyndon, 73
Johnson, Samantha, 94
Jones, W. T., 141

Kane, Jean, 106–8, 115
Kant, Immanuel, 85, 91, 138–39
Kass, Leon, 115
Kelly, Midge, 116–18, 126, 127
Kennedy, Sarah, 67–68, 70
Kresnick, Fred, 106–8

Laurie, 81–83, 91
Lewis, C. S., 37
Lucas, J. R., 45, 105
Lyons, David, 39

MacIlhaney, Mrs., 17
MacIntyre, Alastair, 141
McWhortle, Mr., 106–8, 115
Mayo, Bernard, 66
Midge Kelly, 116–18, 126, 127
Mill, John Stuart, 28, 35, 138
Moore, G. E., 37, 139, 140
Myrna, 83

Nagel, Thomas, 92, 104
Narveson, Jan, 80
Neilsen, Kai, 127
Newton, Lisa H., 105
Nietzsche, Frederick, 139
Norris, Dr., 81–82

Orr, John B., 129
Orwell, George, 95

Paul, 41
Paul, King, 29
Paul, St., 39
Perkins, Fred, 1–3, 14
Peter, 41
Peter, Prince, 28–32
Plato, 15, 89, 124, 132, 133, 134
Price, Richard, 137
Prichard, H. A., 29, 66
Purtill, Richard L., 79

Rachels, James, 80, 92, 104
Ramsey, Paul, 80
Rand, Ayn, 24, 27
Rashdall, Hastings, 66
Rawls, John, 112
Regan, Tom, 80
Reid, Thomas, 137
Rescher, Nicholas, 80
Rose, 71–72
Ross, W. D., 15, 45–46, 51, 52, 126, 128, 138, 140
Ruddick, Sara, 92

Samantha Johnson, 94
Sam Shapiro, 16–18, 26
Sanders, Pierce, 93–94, 98–99, 104
Schiller, Fredericka, 94
Schopenhauer, Arthur, 139
Scrooge, Mr., 56–57
Sellars, Wilfred, 27, 38, 129
Shapiro, Sam, 16–18, 26
Sidgewick, Henry, 38, 66, 138, 141
Singer, Marcus, 38
Singer, Peter, 115
Smart, J. C. C., 35–36
Smith, Frank, 16–18, 26
Sobel, Howard, 3–7
Socrates, 24, 132
Spinoza, 138
Steve, 81–83
Stevenson, C. L., 15, 139
Sue, 2–3

Ted, 40–41, 44
Thompson, Judith Jarvis, 80, 105
Tom Brown, 40–41, 44–45
Toulmin, Stephan, 128

Van Der Haag, Ernest, 80
Vincent, 71–72
Von Vogt, A. E., 71

Warnock, G. J., 38, 127, 128, 141
Warren, Mary Anne, 80
Wasserstrom, Richard, 80, 92
Wellman, Carl, 15, 128
Wells, Donald, 80
Wesley, John, 136
Williams, James, 93–94
Wright, George Henryk von, 140